Interpretive Autoethnography

Interpretive Autoethnography

Second Edition

Norman K. Denzin

University of Illinois at Urbana-Champaign

Los Angeles | London | New Delhi
Singapore | Washington DC

Los Angeles | London | New Delhi
Singapore | Washington DC

FOR INFORMATION:

SAGE Publications, Inc.
2455 Teller Road
Thousand Oaks, California 91320
E-mail: order@sagepub.com

SAGE Publications Ltd.
1 Oliver's Yard
55 City Road
London EC1Y 1SP
United Kingdom

SAGE Publications India Pvt. Ltd.
B 1/I 1 Mohan Cooperative Industrial Area
Mathura Road, New Delhi 110 044
India

SAGE Publications Asia-Pacific Pte. Ltd.
3 Church Street
#10-04 Samsung Hub
Singapore 049483

Printed in the United States of America

Library of Congress Cataloging-in-Publication Data

Denzin, Norman K.

Interpretive autoethnography / Norman K. Denzin, University of Illinois at Urbana-Champaign.

pages cm.

Includes bibliographical references and index.

ISBN 978-1-4522-9981-5 (pbk. : alk. paper)

1. Ethnology—Biographical methods. 2. Ethnology—Authorship. 3. Autobiography. I. Title.

GN346.6.D46 2014
809′.93592—dc23   2013030679

This book is printed on acid-free paper.

Acquisitions Editor: Helen Salmon
Editorial Assistant: Kaitlin Coghill
Production Editor: Laura Barrett
Copy Editor: Sarah J. Duffy
Typesetter: C&M Digitals (P) Ltd.
Proofreader: Stefanie Storholt
Indexer: Rick Hurd
Cover Designer: Karine Hovsepian
Marketing Manager: Nicole Elliott

MIX
Paper from responsible sources
FSC® C014174
www.fsc.org

13 14 15 16 17 10 9 8 7 6 5 4 3 2 1

Contents

You write in order to change the world, knowing perfectly well you probably can't but also knowing that...the world changes according to the way people see it, and if you alter, even by a millimeter, the way... people look at reality, then you can change it.

James Arthur Baldwin

Preface

C. Wright Mills (1959) is a good place to start:[1]

> The sociological imagination enables us to grasp history and biography and the relations between the two in society. The challenge is to develop a methodology that allows us to examine how the private troubles of individuals are connected to public issues and to public responses to these troubles. That is its task and its promise. Individuals can understand their own experience and gauge their own fate only by locating themselves within their historical moment period. (pp. 5–6, slight paraphrase)

> Performance is the explanation and explication of life itself. (Turner, 1986a, p. 21)

> It is in the *coformativity of meaning with others* that I find myself as a performative autoethnographic researcher. (Spry, 2011, p. 39, italics in original)

In 1989, when the first edition of *Interpretive Biography* was published, the social science literature on life story, biographical methods did not contain any extended treatment of the interpretive point of view. Nor was there any serious attempt to apply this perspective to the study of personal troubles and turning-point moments in the lives of interacting individuals. *Interpretive Biography* and its companion, *Interpretive Interactionism* (Denzin, 2001) were intended to fill this void (see also Denzin, 1997, 2003, 2010). These works remain designed to provide students and scholars with an accessible description of the critical, existential, interpretive approach as has been practiced by myself and others.

This new edition of *Interpretive Biography*, now renamed *Interpretive Autoethnography*, continues the themes of the first edition. But where to begin? In 1989 much of the literature I cite in this revision had not yet been written. Indeed in the last two decades there has been an astounding proliferation of interpretive (auto)biographical methods, what Richardson (2000b, p. 929) calls CAP, or creative analytic practices. These practices build on and move beyond the classic versions of life story, biographical case studies, the topics of the first edition.

These new forms include narrative ethnography, meta-autoethnography (Ellis, 2009, p. 12), autoethnography (Jones, Adams, & Ellis, 2013), collaborative autoethnography (Chang, Ngunjiri, & Hernandez, 2013), co-constructed decolonizing autoethnography (Diversi & Moreira, 2009), duoethnography (Norris & Sawyer, 2012), collaborative writing (Wyatt, Gale, Gannnon, & Davies, 2011), ethnodrama (Saldana, 2011), performance ethnography (Conquergood, 1998; Denzin, 2003; Spry, 2011), sociopoetics (Pelias, 2011), performance writing (Pelias, 1999, 2004; Pollock, 1998b), writing stories (Richardson, 2000b), ethnographic fiction, polyvocal texts, and mystories (Richardson, 2000b; Ulmer, 1989).

Ironically, as these new life story forms take shape, the key terms that define them—*narrative, meaning, voice, experience, reflexivity, presence*, and *representation*—are put under erasure by a new generation of critics. For critics these terms are regarded as leftovers from an age of humanistic inquiry that uncritically valorized the self and its social experiences (Jackson & Mazzei, 2009, 2012; MacLure, 2011, 2012, 2013; Pollock, 2009; Scott, 1992; St. Pierre & Pillow, 2000; more on this later).

While criticisms mount, online representations of life experiences proliferate. Virtual selves with their life stories are everywhere present. The mobile social media technologies make this possible.[2] Untroubled by contemporary critics who challenge terms like *voice* and *presence*, indigenous persons in colonized spaces turn to oral history, myth, and performance narratives to make sense of their lives, themselves, and their collective histories. Words, rituals, and performances matter for them (L. T. Smith, 2012).

The biographical, life history, case study, case history, ethnographic method has been a part of traditional, humanistic interpretive social science discourse since the 1920s and 1930s, when University of Chicago sociologists, under the influence of Park, Thomas, Znaniecki and Burgess, Blumer and Hughes were trained in the qualitative, interpretive, interactionist approach to human group life (see Van Maanen, 2011, pp. 17–22). Sociologists in succeeding generations turned away from the method. They gave their attention to problems of measurement, validity, reliability, responses to attitude questionnaires, survey methodologies, laboratory experiments, theory development, and conceptual indicators. Many researchers combined these interests and problems with the use of the qualitative, life history–biographical method (see Chapter 5 for a discussion of criteria). The result often produced a mixed-method, qualitative-quantitative trivialization and distortion of the original intents of the method.

In the 1970s and 1980s, sociologists and scholars in other disciplines evidenced a renewed interest in the biographical method. In 1978, a Biography and Sociology group formed within the International Sociological Association

(ISA) and met in Uppsala, Sweden. In 1986, that group became a research committee within the ISA.[3] The Biography and Society group now publishes its own newsletter and journal, *Life Stories/Récits de Vie*. The journal of the Oral History Society, *Oral History,* regularly publishes life history–biographical materials, as does *Auto/Biography*. Autoethnographers regularly post to the Autoethnography Listserv.

In education, communications, sociology, and anthropology a host of journals regularly publish evocative, narrative, literary, autoethnographic texts, including *Text and Performance Quarterly, Qualitative Inquiry, International Review of Qualitative Research, Journal of Loss and Trauma, Anthropology and Humanism Quarterly, Cultural Studies–Critical Methodologies, Signs, Sexualities, Women and Language, Narrative, Narrative Inquiry, Life Writing, Identity, Biography, Auto/Biography*, and *Qualitative Communication Research*. Left Coast Press, in its Social Justice and Writing Lives series, regularly publishes monographs using evocative forms of writing that blur the boundaries between humanities and social sciences. In short, interpretive first person texts have returned to the human disciplines.

The last three decades have seen a resurgence of interest in interpretive approaches to the study of culture, biography, and human group life. Central to this view has been the argument that societies, cultures, and the expressions of human experience can be read as social texts, that is, as structures of representation that require symbolic statement (Clifford & Marcus, 1986; Panourgia & Marcus, 2008; Van Maanen, 2011). These texts, whether oral or written, have taken on a problematic status in the interpretive project (Conquergood, 1998). Questions have emerged concerning how texts are authored, read, and interpreted (Derrida, 1972/1981). How authors, lives, societies, and cultures get inside interpretive texts is now a hotly debated topic (Geertz, 1988). The central assumption of the interpretive (auto)biographical method—that a life can be captured and represented in a text—is now open to question. A life is a social text, a fictional, narrative production. I address this issue, which has been given the term *the metaphysics of presence* (Derrida, 1972/1981), throughout this work.

This project takes its direction from three sources: C. Wright Mills (1959), Jean-Paul Sartre (1971/1981), and recent development in literary, interpretive theory (Derrida, 1972/1981). C. Wright Mills argued that the sociological imagination "enables us to grasp history and biography and the relations between the two within society" (p. 6). He then suggested that "no social study that does not come back to the problems of biography, of history and of their intersections within a society has completed its intellectual journey" (p. 6).

In the preface to Volume 1 of *The Family Idiot: Gustave Flaubert, 1821–1857* (1971/1981, pp. ix–x), Jean-Paul Sartre asks (paraphrase):

Where to start? We must find that project, act, event, that gives primary meaning to the person's life, that event the subject seeks to understand the most. This experience gives primary meaning to the person' life. We must discover that event and see how it embeds the person in their historical moment, then we can work back into history.

Sartre's method, earlier set out in his *Search for a Method* (1963), provides a connection to Mills's injunction.

New Directions for Interpretive Autoethnography

It is time to chart a new course, time to explore a new set of terms. I want to turn the traditional life story, biographical project into an interpretive autoethnographic project, into a critical, performative practice, a practice that begins with the biography of the writer and moves outward to culture, discourse, history, and ideology.

Interpretive performance autoethnography allows the researcher to take up each person's life in its immediate particularity and to ground the life in its historical moment. We move back and forth in time, using a version of Sartre's (1963, pp. 85–166) progressive-regressive method (see also Norris & Sawyer, 2012, p. 12; Pinar, 1975). Interpretation works forward to the conclusion of a set of acts taken up by the subject while working back in time, interrogating the historical, cultural, and biographical conditions that moved the person to experience the events being studied (Denzin, 2001 p. 41).[4] These events occur in those sites where structure, history, and autobiography intersect.

Ulmer's (1989, p. 209) concept of mystory, combined with the notion of epiphany (Denzin, 2001, p. 34), sharpens the focus. Performance and interpretation work outward from turning-point events in a person's life. The sting of memory defines these events. They become part of the person' mystory, part of his or her interpretive autoethnography.

With Sartre and Ulmer there is a political component to interpretive autoethnography, a commitment to a social justice agenda—to inquiry that explicitly addresses issues of inequity and injustice in particular social moments and places.

In this book I want to outline the basic features and concepts of this approach, connecting the dots between lives, performance, representation, epiphanies, and interpretation. I weave my narrative through family stories. I conclude with thoughts concerning a performance-centered pedagogy and the directions, concerns, and challenges for autoethnography.

A basic question drives the interpretive project in the human disciplines: How do men and women give meaning to their lives and perform these meanings in their daily lives? There is a pressing demand to show how the practices of critical, interpretive, qualitative research can help change the world in positive ways.

As Marx (1852/1983, p. 287) observed, men and women "make their own history, but not . . . under conditions they have chosen for themselves; rather on terms immediately existing, given and handed down to them." Our project is to interpret and change the conditions under which lives are lived.

Chapter 1 examines key assumptions of the biographical approach. A select number of texts are presented. I draw on recent literary statements on the theory of the autobiography. Chapter 2 defines key terms, including *autobiography, biography, life story, self story, case study, case history, fiction, narrative, history, oral history,* and *personal history.* Chapter 3 discusses guidelines for gathering and interpreting biographical materials. Chapter 4 takes up the concept of epiphany, or turning-point moments in persons' lives. It analyzes some personal experience and self stories. It examines stories within stories and the group locus of stories. Chapter 5, addresses the problem of writing and reading performance texts. Chapter 6 discusses obituaries and returns to performance autoethnography's primary purpose, which is to help us make sense of our fragmented lives.

Notes

1. I altered the pronouns in Mills's text, changing *his* to *their.*

2. The technologies take many forms, from video and audio recordings made on smartphones to Skype encounters; YouTube, Facebook, and Twitter postings; discussions in online recovery groups; to Internet forums, blogs, wikis, podcasts, and LinkedIn exchanges. These technologies allow persons in virtual communities to share information about themselves, their biographies, and their intimate experiences. Virtual selves have material presences in these electronic spaces.

3. See Bertaux and Kohli (1984) for a history of the group. Since 1984 this group—Research Committee 38: Biography and Society—has been a formal RC within the International Sociological Association. The 35th anniversary of the RC was held in Lodz, Poland, June 17–18, 2013.

4. Norris and Sawyer's (2012, p. 12) concept of duoethnography extends Pinar, who also uses Sartre's progressive-regressive method. Each person's life can be read, forward and backward in time, as a curriculum, as a set of performative skills, knowledges, and pedagogical practices (more on this later).

Acknowledgments

I would like to thank Peter K. Manning, John Van Maanen, and Mitch Allen for launching the first edition, and Helen Salmon and the following reviewers for helping me shape this revision:

Tony E. Adams, Northeastern Illinois University

Christine S. Davis, University of North Carolina at Charlotte

Christopher N. Poulos, University of North Carolina at Greensboro

Tami Spry, St. Cloud State University

Lois McFadyen Christensen, University of Alabama at Birmingham

Graham Smart, Carleton University

I would also like to thank my wife, Katherine E. Ryan, who helped give this book whatever coherence it may have, and Sarah Duffy and Stefanie Storholt for assistance in copyediting and proofreading.

About the Author

Norman K. Denzin is Distinguished Professor of Communications, College of Communications Scholar, and Research Professor of Communications, Sociology, and Humanities at the University of Illinois, Urbana-Champaign. He is the author or editor of more than two dozen books, including *Indians on Display, Custer on Canvas, The Qualitative Manifesto, Qualitative Inquiry Under Fire, Searching for Yellowstone, Reading Race, Interpretive Ethnography, The Cinematic Society, The Voyeur's Gaze*, and *The Alcoholic Self*. He is past editor of *The Sociological Quarterly*, co-editor (with Yvonna S. Lincoln) of four editions of the *Handbook of Qualitative Research*, coeditor (with Michael D. Giardina) of eight plenary volumes from the annual Congress of Qualitative Inquiry, co-editor (with Lincoln) of the methods journal *Qualitative Inquiry*, founding editor of *Cultural Studies/Critical Methodologies* and *International Review of Qualitative Research*, and editor of three book series.

1   Assumptions of the Method

If we trace our roots to the classic Greek value of participation in civic life, [then] performance is a means and mechanism for embodying our individual responsibilities to community and an ethics of participation. (Jones, 2013, p. 78)

Pentimento: Something painted out of a picture which later becomes visible again.

Conventional distinctions between performance and text—the telling and the told, the act of saying and the what is said, action and meaning—fall away in favor of a dynamic reconception of texts as inseparable from the processes by which they are made, understood, and deployed. (Pollock, 1998a, p. 21, paraphrase; see also Rusted, 2006, p. 117)

Lives and their experiences, the telling and the told, are represented in stories which are performances. Stories are like pictures that have been painted over, and, when paint is scraped off an old picture, something new becomes visible. What is new is what was previously covered up. A life and the performances about it have the qualities of *pentimento*. Something new is always coming into sight, displacing what was previously certain and seen. There is no truth in the painting of a life, only multiple images and traces of what has been, what could have been, and what now is. There is no firm distinction between the texts and performances.

The subject matter of interpretive autoethnography is the life experiences and performances of a person. In this chapter I outline the basic features and concepts of this approach, connecting the dots between lives, performance, representation, epiphany, and interpretation. But first a brief aside on history.

The Subject and the Autoethnographic Method

From its birth, modern, qualitative, interpretive sociology—which I date with Weber's (1922/1947) meditations on *verstehen* and method—has been haunted by a *metaphysics of presence* (Derrida, 1972, p. 250), which asserts that real, concrete subjects live lives with meaning and these meanings have a concrete presence in the lives of these people.[1] This belief in a real subject who is present in the world has led sociologists to continue to search for a method (Sartre, 1963) that would allow them to uncover how these subjects give subjective meaning to their life experiences (Schutz, 1932/1967). This method would rely on the subjective verbal and written expressions of meaning given by the individuals being studied, these expressions being windows into the inner life of the person. Since Dilthey (1900/1976), this search has led to a perennial focus in the human sciences on the (auto)biographical approach and its interpretive variants, including hermeneutics.[2]

Derrida (1972) has contributed to the understanding that there is no clear window into the inner life of a person, for any window is always filtered through the glaze of language, signs, and the process of signification. And language, in both its written and spoken forms, is always inherently unstable, in flux, and made up of the traces of other signs and symbolic statements. Hence there can never be a clear, unambiguous statement of anything, including an intention or a meaning.

A cautionary note: Experience, lived and otherwise, is discursively constructed. It is not a foundational category. There is no empirically stable I giving a true account of an experience. Experience has no existence apart from the storied acts of performative-I (Pollock, 2007, p. 240; Scott, 1992).

My task in this book is to reconcile this concern with the metaphysics of presence, and its representations with a commitment to the position that interpretive social science scholars study real flesh-and-blood people who have real-life experiences in the social world.

Exemplar

Here is an example. Yvonna S. Lincoln (2002) writes about grieving immediately after the attacks on the World Trade Center and the Pentagon on September 11, 2001:

> For two weeks now, we have watched the staggering outpouring of grief, shock and horror as a nation struggles to come to terms with the attacks. . . . And I, too, have sat numb with shock, glued to the television screen, struggling with the incomprehensibility of these acts, overwhelmed by the bewildering world view which could have led

people to commit such atrocities. But I have been numb for another reason, and it will be important to see my reasons as another part of the phenomenon which has struck so deeply at the heart and soul of the United States. I sat numb because my reactions to grief are always usually private. They are always delayed....

My people—my family (of English and Dutch and Scottish stock) were born and raised, as were their parents before them, in the southern Appalachian mountains.... Mountain people... keep their emotions to themselves, especially those of a most private nature.... The end result, I have come to realize, is a human being who lives with his or her grief for all their days. The future, like tears, never comes. (p. 147)

Lincoln writes herself into this historical space. She reads her emotions through her family history. Her people keep their emotions to themselves. Epiphanies, like Lincoln's, are the subject matter of interpretive autoethnography.

And here is a second example, why Claudio Moreira (2012) hates chicken breast:

Sister and I sit in the kitchen having dinner...a man sits at the head of the table....A man with his beer....I keep my eyes down, teasing the piece of chicken on my plate. Usually Sister and I share the breast of the chicken but not today. It does not matter who paid for the bird. It does not matter for how long, since yesterday or last month, we have been without any kind of meat on our table. The best and most expensive part of the chicken belongs to the man... and the man does not share.

There are different rules when this man is at the house. Sister and I learn the rules; we learn to dislike chicken breast....I am nine years old and this is one of the strongest memories I will have from this man I call Father. I was nine when I decided I hate chicken breast. (pp. 151–152)

This is a resistance narrative, an autoethnographic story that resists and demands telling at the same time. It is a story written and performed from a place of pain, a writing self writing as a performative I, an I, a self that resists, tells, escapes, feels.

Claudio:

Typing those words you have just quoted, I have a hard time to eat. I can tell you about this burning feeling like a vomit I cannot hold. I am trying to explore possibilities of writing where visceral knowledge can exist in all its physicality. (p. 163)

This is performative writing, a decolonizing autoethnography.

Claudio:

I am trying to write in a way that embodies my sociological imagination, I am trying to historicize my body, with its muscles, blood, anger, and hunger. I'm rewriting my life story to create the conditions for changing myself and my past. (p. 158, paraphrase)

What Stories Should Have

Stories, as performances, follow conventions. They typically have these elements:

1. People depicted as characters

2. A scene, place, or context where the story occurs

3. An epiphany or crisis that provides dramatic tension, around which the emplotted events depicted in the story revolve and toward which a resolution is pointed

4. A temporal order of events

5. A point or moral to the story which gives meaning to the experiences depicted (Bochner & Riggs, in press)

Writing Trauma, Performing Lives

The storied performances of life experiences move outward from the selves of the person and inward to the persons and groups that give them meaning and structure. Persons are arbitrators of their own presence in the world, and they should have the last word on this problem. Our texts must always return to and reflect the words persons speak as they attempt to give meaning and shape to the lives they lead. The materials of the autoethnographic project resolve, in the final analysis, into the stories persons perform with and for one another.

Jean O'Malley Halley (2012, pp. 86–87) says of her story:

My story, as told, mimics the lived experience of trauma circling around and through tone, place, and familial generations.... I repeat scenes, and in particular one scene involving my sister and me, again and again....I use repetition...as a means to express trauma. In my memoir writing, repetition happens at the sentence level, the same words said two or three times in two or three sentences again and again....

Trauma cuts through time and reoccurs as a compulsive repetition of the traumatic moment, of the violence.... I tell my childhood story much as it was and continues to be experienced by me. . . .

It was late at night. And we were little girls.. My sister loved that cat. She loved that cat. Really, she had not much else to love. And he [father] woke us up. And he brought us to the garage. I don't remember getting there. Instead, suddenly in my mind, it is night and we are there, my sister and I, standing side by side.... In remembering how, 33 years ago, my father gutted my sister's beloved childhood cat in front of us in a drunken rage...these repetitions...the violence it grips me and again and again and again, sweeping over me...that night when he killed my sister's cat...he shouted at us..."I am a Man! I am a man!

Just as Claudio's father was a man.

Memories of trauma are connected to psychic, physical, and sexual violence. The memories are experienced moments of epiphany which are repeated over and over again. That is, as Halley notes, trauma is experienced as repetition; the memories, images, and emotions will not go away. The use of repetition, at the sentence level, mirrors the trauma experience.

Clough (2007, pp. 5–7, 13) writes on the importance of trauma:

> In the last years of the twentieth century, critical theory came to focus on trauma, loss and melancholy.... [I]n taking up trauma, critical theory was able to transition ...to new forms of history often presented at first in autobiographical experimental writings.... [T]hese writings...call into question the truth of representation, the certainty of memory, if not the possibility of knowledge of the past....
>
> The experimental forms of writing that mean to capture trauma often present the subject in blanks, hesitations—a topographic formulation of forgetting, loss, uncertainty, disavowal, and defensiveness.... [T]rauma makes the past and the future meet without there being a present. The future is collapsed into the past as the past overwhelms the present.

Or, as Halley (2012) writes, trauma is written in the gendered spaces of hesitation, violence, forgetting, and repetition. Both "violence and trauma produce and reproduce gendered social power" (p. 89). In writing about trauma, violence, and betrayal, in reliving the trauma, Halley, like Claudio, was pushed forward, out of the violence, into something else. She lived her way forward, out of the past back to the present (p. 12), as did Claudio.

Stories of loss and pain are learned and told in cultural groups. The stories that members of groups pass on to one another are reflective of repressed and distorted understandings and practices that are at work in the larger systems of cultural discourse. But then there are only stories to be told and (hopefully) listened to.

I am a Man, Jean's father shouts. And in those words he tells his story. He is a man who kills animals. Stories like his resolve the dilemmas surrounding the metaphysics of presence. One becomes the stories one tells. This is who Jean's father is. A MAN! The elusive, but brute force of his story calls us back to the understanding that this business of a life story is just that, a story that can never be completed, a storied set of performances trapped in repetitive loops which produce pain and trauma for others.

Stories Then...

Stories, then, like the lives they tell about, are always open-ended, inconclusive, and ambiguous, subject to multiple interpretations. Some are big; others are little. Some take on heroic, folktale proportions in the cultural lives of group members; others are tragic; and all too few are comic. Some break fast and run to rapid conclusions. Most slowly unwind and twist back on themselves as persons seek to find meaning for themselves in the experiences they call their own. Some are told for the person by others who are called experts, be these journalists or professional biographers. Some the person keeps to himself or herself and tells no one else. Many individuals are at a loss as to what story to tell, feeling that they have nothing worthwhile to talk about. Within this group, there are persons who have no voice and no one to tell their story to.

This means that autoethnographic work must always be interventionist, seeking to give notice to those who may otherwise not be allowed to tell their story or who are denied a voice to speak. This is what Écriture féminine, radical feminist discourse, and critical theory attempt, a radical form of writing which "transgresses structures of domination—a kind of writing which reproduces the struggle for voice of those on the wrong side of the power relationship" (Clough, 1988, p. 3; see also Clough, 2007, p. 6; Halley, 2012, pp. 88–89). This stance disrupts the classic oedipal logic of the life history method which situated subjectivity and self-development in the patriarchal system of marriage, kinship, and sexuality. Écriture féminine, moving from a deconstructive stance, makes no attempt at the production of biographical narratives which fill out the sociologist's version of what a life and its stories should look like. It accepts sociology as fictive writing and biographical work as the search for partial, not full, identities (Clough, 1988, p. 14).

Ultimately, the writer may abandon ethnographies of the other and turn to autoethnography. Clough (1990) states, "I made a choice to abandon the writing of ethnography of other women. I choose instead to set out again to know myself as a woman, as a woman writer" (p. 42).

We must learn how to connect (auto)biographies and lived experiences, the epiphanies of lives, to the groups and social relationships that surround and shape persons. As we write about lives, we bring the world of others into our texts. We create differences, oppositions, and presences which allow us to maintain the illusion that we have captured the "real" experiences of "real" people. In fact, we create the persons we write about, just as they create themselves when they engage in storytelling practices.

We must become more sensitive to the writing strategies we use when we attempt to accomplish these ends. And, as readers, we can only have trust or mistrust in the writers that we read, for there is no way to stuff a real-live person between the two covers of a text. As we learn to do this, we must remember that our primary obligation is always to the people we study, not to our project or to a larger discipline.

Situating the Method

Autoethnographies and biographies are conventionalized, narrative expressions of life experiences. These conventions, which structure how life experiences are performed, told, and written about, involve the following problematic presuppositions and taken-for-granted assumptions: (1) the existence of others; (2) the influence and importance of race, gender, and class; (3) family beginnings; (4) turning points; (5) known and knowing authors and observers; (6) objective life markers; (7) real persons with real lives; (8) turning-point experiences; and (9) truthful statements distinguished from fictions.

These conventions serve to define the autoethnographic method as a distinct approach to the study of human experience. They are the methods by which the "real" appearances of "real" people are created. They are Western literary conventions and have been present since the invention of the (auto)biographical form. Some are more central than others, although they all appear to be universal, while they change and take different form depending on the writer, the place of writing, and the historical moment. They shape how lives are told, performed, and understood. In so doing, they create the subject matter of the autoethnographic approach.

The "Other": Autoethnographic texts are always written (and performed) with an "other" in mind. This other may be Jean's father, Claudio's father and Sister, or Yvonna's family. The presence of an other in autobiographical and biographical texts means that they are always written with at least a double perspective in mind: the author's and the other's. The eye of the other directs the eye of the writer (Elbaz, 1987, p. 14).

Gender, Race, and Class: These texts are raced, gendered, class productions, reflecting the biases and values of racism, patriarchy, and the middle class. They are ideological statements. Anna J. Cooper (1858–1964), feminist, human rights advocate, educational reformer, daughter of a slave woman, writes of her ancestors:

> The part of my ancestors that did not come over in the Mayflower in 1620, arrived, I am sure year earlier in the Fateful Dutch trader that out in at Jamestown in 1619.... I believe that the third source of my individual stream comes... [f]rom the vanishing Red Men, which I ought... to the manner born and "inheritor of the globe" [make me a] genuine F. F. F. (First Family of America). (quoted in Hutchinson, 1981, p. 3)

Family Beginnings: These productions are grounded in the traumas of family, family history, and the presences and absences of mothers and fathers.

It is as if every author of an autobiography or biography must start with family, finding there the zero point of origin for the life in question. Elbaz (1987, p. 70) argues that, by the 18th century, "this concept of zero point had extended from the realm of the individual self to that of the social whole." Davis (1986, pp. 53–54) suggests that, in 16th century France, the family system played a double function of placing persons within a patriarchal structure while positioning them within a larger social field. These "family" others are seen as having major structuring effects on the life being written about.

Vine Deloria (1997, pp. 35–36), Sioux Indian and author of *Custer Died for Your Sins* (1969), discusses his family history, his father, and his education:

> I grew up on the Pine Ridge reservation in South Dakota ... about thirty miles from Wounded Knee. ... I went to grade school, half white, and half mixed-blooded Indians. They taught us Rudyard Kipling's world view. It was a simplistic theory ... the United States has never been in the wrong side of anything. The Government has never lied to the people. ... It was a glossed-over history. ... My father was an Episcopal missionary on the reservation. His father was too. ... Our family was one of the first to move from the old ways to the white man's ways. [But] mine was a long tradition of medicine men. ... My father knew all kinds of medicine songs and stories. He held on to the two cultures without, much conflict until the late sixties. ... The church put tremendous pressure on the Indians to integrate. He said: "We don't have to. We can [be] what we are without getting into the melting pot."

Textual Turning Points: By beginning the autoethnographic or biographical text with family, these sources presume that lives have beginnings or starting points. But, on this, Gertrude Stein reminds us:

> About six weeks ago Gertrude Stein said, it does not look to me as if you were ever going to write that autobiography. You know what I am going to do. I am going to write it for you. I am going to write it as simply as Defoe did the autobiography of Robinson Crusoe. And she has and this is it. (quoted in Elbaz, 1987, p. 13)

This passage appears at the end of Stein's (1933) *The Autobiography of Alice B. Toklas*. Stein is telling the reader that "the beginning coincides with the end and the end with the beginning—which is the end—for autobiography (like fiction) is an act of ceaseless renewal: the story is never 'told' finally, exhaustively, completely" (quoted in Elbaz, 1987, p. 13). Stein is suggesting that the narrator or writer of an autoethnography is a fiction. That is, just as Defoe wrote a fictional autobiography of a fictional character, Robinson Crusoe, Stein has written a fictional autobiography of herself called *The Autobiography of Alice B. Toklas*. Stein is contending that the line between lives and fictions is impossibly and unnecessarily drawn (see discussion below). Still, the autoethnographic, autobiographical, and biographical genres are structured by the belief that lives have beginnings in families. Since this belief is part of the genre, virtually all biographical texts begin with family history. Stein's position challenges this conventional view concerning beginnings.

Knowing Authors: These texts presume the presence of a writer who can record and make sense of the life in question. If the text is autobiographical, it is assumed that the self of the writer knows his or her life, and hence is in the best position to write about it.

Objective Markers: Lives have objective and subjective markers, and these markers reflect key, critical points about the life and person in question. They suggest the existence of "real" persons, whose existence in a real world can be mapped, charted, and given meaning. It is assumed that these markers fit into place and give coherence to the life in question. Sartre (1971/1981, p. ix), in his discussion of Flaubert's life, makes the following argument as he describes two pieces of information about Flaubert:

> The fragments of information we have are very different in *kind;* Flaubert was born in December 1821 . . . that is one kind of information. . . . [H]e writes, much later, to his mistress: "Art terrifies me"—that is another. The first is an objective, social fact, confirmed by official documents; the second, objective too . . . refers in its meaning to a feeling that issues from experience. . . . Do we not then risk ending up with layers of heterogeneous and irreducible meanings? This book attempts to prove that irreducibility is only apparent, and that each piece of data set in its place becomes a portion of the whole, which is constantly being created, and by the same token reveals its profound homogeneity with all the other parts that make up the whole.

A life, it is assumed, is cut of whole cloth, and its many pieces, with careful scrutiny, can be fitted into proper place. But this writing/performing of a life, Sartre suggests, like Stein, is constantly being created as it is written/performed. Hence the meanings of the pieces change as new patterns are found.

The Subject in the Text: An Aside

Sartre's position skirts the problem of the subject's "reality" in the world of the autoethnographic text. Granted, Flaubert was born in December 1821, but how does Sartre get Flaubert's life into his text? This is the problem of language and writing, for, as Derrida (1972/1981) argues, the principle knowledge of (and about) a subject only exists in the texts written about them. Sartre proclaims the existence of a "real" person, Flaubert. However, as Benveniste (1966) argues, and Derrida (1972/1981, p. 29; 1972) develops, the linguistic concept of *person* or *subject* in language refers only to the person making an utterance, as in "I am writing this line about persons." My referentiality in this line is only given in the pronoun *I*. My personhood is not in this line. The pronoun *I* is a shifter, and its only reference is in the discourse that surrounds it. This means, as Elbaz (1987, p. 6) argues, that "the notion of person takes meaning only within the parameters of the discursive event." My existence, or Flaubert's, is primarily and discursively documented in the words written about or by them.

But more is involved than just the use of personal pronouns like *I*. Persons as speaking subjects (Merleau-Ponty, 1964, p. 84) are not just empty signs, created solely by the syntactical and semiological structures of language (Ricoeur, 1974, pp. 236–266).[3] Language, for the biographer and autobiographer, is not just an object or a structure "but a mediation through which and by means of which" (Ricoeur, 1974, p. 251) writers and speakers are directed toward biographically meaningful reality. What is at issue here is how the writing and speaking subject, as "the bearer of meaning" in his or her texts, appropriates this pronoun *I*, which is an empty sign, and "posits himself [or herself] in expressing himself [or herself]" (Ricoeur, 1974, pp. 246, 256).

The pronoun *I* is performative; it is waiting to be used by the autobiographical subject. Indeed, the genre and the larger political economy where such texts circulate dictates its use, along with its referent, *self* (see Elbaz, 1987, p. 153). But, as Benveniste (1966, p. 218) observes, "I signifies the person who is uttering the present instance of the discourse containing I." Now, while any speaker or writer can use this empty sign, when it is used by the writer of a biographical or autobiographical text, its use signifies *this* person making *this* utterance, *this* claim, or *this* statement. Behind the pronoun stands a named person—a person with a biography. When, as a writer and a speaker, this person appropriates these words and this pronoun (*I, you, he, she, me*), he or she brings the full weight of his or her personal biography to bear on the utterance or statement in question (see Schutz & Luckmann, 1973, p. 114). The personal pronoun thus signifies this person making this utterance. It becomes a historical claim, a writing and speaking event. It is a performance that simultaneously embodies and makes theory and experience visible to others (Pelias, 1999, p. xi).

Performative writing, as when I type these words that you are now reading, is embodied, evocative, always inconclusive and open-ended (Pollock, 1998b, 1998c, 2007). It is nervous writing, it hesitates and stutters, moving from one charged moment to the next, with a sense of urgency (Pollock, 1998b, p. 91; 1998c, p. 43).

This is what autobiographies and biographies are all about: writers making biographical claims about their ability to make biographical and autobiographical statements about themselves and others. In this way, the personal pronouns take on semantic and not just syntactic and semiological meanings (Ricoeur, 1974, p. 256). The self and its signifiers (*I,* etc.) thus take on a double existence in the biographical text. First, they point inward to the text itself, where they are arranged within a system of autobiographical narrative. Second, they point outward to this life that has been led by this writer or this subject. In performativity action turns back on itself and the actor sees double. Untangling this mediation and interaction between text, performer, and performance is what the above discussion has been all about.

Tami Spry:

I sit left of center stage in a straight-backed wooden chair with No arms. Pieces of paper lie scattered around me.... From where I sit, I can read some of the pieces. There are words or bits of words forming a grammar of fear and confusion. Agitated, I rise from the chair. My arms break off my shoulders and bounce stiff and clumsy about my anklets on the stage. I stumble trying to assemble the shards of this language, fractured fairy tales from the wreckage of a birth and death.

I lurch within the boundaries of the stage trying to read the pieces, trying to remember sentence structure, trying to piece together an alphabet. (Spry, 2011, p. 27)

This is performative autoethnography, the performative-I on stage. Straight-back in a wooden chair "words fall away, we lurch back and forth within confines of this chair, we yank our bodies back in line, only to stumble off stage as we are gripped by fear" (Spry, 2011, p. 27, paraphrase). This us embodied, critical pedagogy, moving from body to paper to stage. Here is where we find real people working at performing themselves for others.

Della Pollock describes seeing Carol Channing performing in *Hello Dolly* at the Auditorium Theatre in Chicago:

There she was, at the top of the winding staircase, one long gloved hand laid along the white balustrade: she was every dame, mame, belle who had ever descended ... a long winding staircase to a waiting chorus of high-kicking men. She and we relished every wigged, lip-sticked, and sequined step, each timed so perfectly that she arrived on the stage apron with the final crescendo of the music, which seemed to rise on our cue, as we rose to clap and clap and clap, performing a standing ovation literally to beat the band. And yet, this was still Dolly—or was it Carol? ...

When a stunned hush finally reigned Carol/Dolly—Dolly/Carol took one more carefully balanced step toward us, bent slightly at the hip, as if to share a secret . . . she spoke with glowing, exaggerated precision in an absolutely delicious stage whisper—"Shall we do that again?" . . . Now the performance launches onto . . . a new plane of repetition . . . that exceeds both the thing done and the doing of it. (Pollock, 2007, pp. 243–244)

The Real Person: When a writer purports to be giving the "real" objective details of a "real" person's life, he or she is, in fact, only creating that subject in the text that is written. To send readers back to a "real" person is to send them back to yet another version of the fiction that is in the text. There is no "real" person behind the text, except as he or she exists in another system of discourse. But the central postulate of the biographical method (and of this book) is that there is a "real" person "out there" who has lived a life, and this life can be written about. This "real" person was born, has perhaps died, has left his or her mark on other people, and has probably deeply felt the human emotions of shame, love, hate, guilt, anger, despair, and caring for others. This feeling, thinking, living, breathing person is the "real" subject of the biographical method.

The languages of autobiographical and biographical texts, then, cannot be taken as mere windows into the "real" world of "real" interacting subjects. These languages are only devices, tools, or *bricolages* for creating texts. The writers who use them are *bricoleurs,* or persons who use the "means at hand" to create texts which look like autobiographies or biographies (Derrida, 1972, p. 255).

Turning Points: Barely hinted at in the above discussion is the belief, already elaborated in the concept of epiphany, that a life is shaped by key turning-point moments. These moments leave permanent marks. Again I draw an example from Sartre, only now from his biography of Jean Genet (1952/1963, p. 1):

An accident riveted him to a childhood memory, and this memory became sacred. In his early childhood, a liturgical drama was performed, a drama of which he was the officiant [one who officiates]: he knew paradise and lost it, he was a child and driven from his childhood. No doubt this "break" is not easy to localize. It shifts back and forth, at the dictates of his moods and myths, between the ages of ten and fifteen. But that is unimportant. What matters is that it exists and that he believes in it. His life is divided into two heterogeneous parts: before and after the sacred drama.

The notion that lives are turned around by significant events, what I called *epiphanies,* is deeply entrenched in Western thought. At least since Augustine, the idea of transformation has been a central part of the autobiographical and biographical form.[4] This means that biographical texts will typically be structured by the significant turning-point moments in a subject's life.

These moments may be as insignificant as Augustine's stealing pears from a pear tree and feeling guilt about the theft (Freccero, 1986, p. 23) or as profoundly moving as the scene in Genet's life described above by Sartre.

Truth: The above texts suggest that lives have objective, factually correct, "truth-like," documentary features. A person was born on such a date, died on this date, and, in between these dates, lived an important life. But facts can be altered by a storyteller in order to make them interesting and more significant. As suggested above, to argue for a factually correct picture of a "real" person is to ignore how persons are created in performances.

Standards of Autobiographical Truth

Various standards of truth or verisimilitude in autobiographies have been proposed.[5] These include sincerity, subjective truth, historical truth, and fictional truth. The sincere autobiographer is assumed to be willing to tell the subjective truths about his or her life. A historically truthful statement would be one that accords with existing empirical data on an event or experience. An aesthetic truth is evidenced when "the autobiography is an aesthetic success" (Kohli, 1987, p. 79). Presumably such a work conforms to the canons of the autobiographical genre and reports the writer's life as the public wants to hear it reported. A fictional truth occurs when it is argued that the "'real' truth is to be contained in 'pure' fiction" (p. 73).

More is at issue, however, than just different types of truth. The problem involves facts, facticities, and fiction. *Facts* refer to events that are believed to have occurred or will occur (e.g., the date today is July 27, 1988). *Facticities* describe how those facts were lived and experienced by interacting individuals (Husserl, 1913/1962, pp. 184, 410; Merleau-Ponty, 1964, p. 119). *Fiction* is a narrative (story, account) which deals with real or imagined facts and facticities. *Truth*, in the present context, refers to statements that are in agreement with facts and facticities as they are known and commonly understood "within a community of minds" (Peirce, 1959, vol. 8, p. 18; 1958, p. 74). *Reality* consists of the "objects, qualities or events to which true ideas are" directed (Peirce, 1958, p. 74). There are, then, true and false fictions, that is, fictions that are in accord with facts and facticities as they are known or have been experienced, and fictions that distort or misrepresent these understandings. A truthful fiction (narrative) is faithful to facticities and facts. It creates verisimilitude, or what are for the reader believable experiences.

Shapiro (1968, p. 425), Pascal (1960, p. 19), and Renza (1977, p. 26) argue that the autobiography is an imaginative organization of experience that imposes a distortion of truth.[6] Autobiographical statements are, then, viewed as a mixture of fiction and nonfiction, for each text contains certain unique truths or verisimilitudes about life and particular lived experiences. Elbaz (1987, p. 11) quotes Renza (1977, p. 26), who claims that autobiographies are neither fictional nor factual:

> We might say...that autobiography is neither fictive nor non-fictive....We might view it...as a unique, self-defining mode of self-referential expression...that allows, then inhibits, the project of self-presentification....Thus we might conceive of autobiographical writing as an endless prelude: a beginning without middle (the realm of fiction), or without end (the realm of history); a purely fragmentary, incomplete literary project, unable to be more than an arbitrary document.

Here, Renza is making an unnecessary distinction between fiction and nonfiction, for all writing, as suggested above, is fictional. His other points about the autobiography warrant discussion. He assumes that there is a real self-referential self that gets expressed in the writer's text, and this self expresses itself in unique ways. What he fails to clarify is that the real self-referential self is only present in a series of discourses about who a person is or was in the past. As Elbaz (1987, p. 12) observes, "The autobiographer always writes a novel, a fiction, about a third person," this third person being who he or she was yesterday, last year, or one hour ago. Autobiography and biography present fictions about "thought" selves, "thought" experiences, events and their meanings. Such works are tormented by the problem of getting this person into the text, of bringing the person alive and making him or her believable. Fictions, in this sense, merely arrange and rearrange events that could have happened or did happen. Realist fiction, for example, presents its narrative in a way that is made to appear factual, that is, as a linear, chronological sequence of events. Elbaz argues, and I agree, "autobiography is fiction and fiction is autobiography: *both are narrative arrangements of reality*" (p. 1, italics added).

The autobiographical and biographical forms, like all writing forms, are always *incomplete* literary productions. They are never arbitrary, as Renza argues, for no documents are ever arbitrary (Elbaz, 1987, p. 12). These two forms are always a series of beginnings, which are then closed or brought to closure through the use of a set of narrative devices. These devices, called conclusions or last chapters, allow these forms to conform with the cultural myth that lives have endings[7] and that true, complete stories about these lives have been or can be told. However, as argued above, autobiographies and biographies are only fictional statements with varying degrees of "truth" about "real" lives. True stories are stories that are believed in.

Autoethnographic and biographical studies should attempt to articulate how each subject deals with the problems of coherence, illusion, consubstantiality, presence, deep inner selves, others, gender, class, starting and ending points, epiphanies, fictions, truths, and final causes. These recurring, obdurate, culturally constructed dimensions of Western lives provide framing devices for the stories that are told about the lives that we study. They are, however, no more than artifices, contrivances that writers and tellers are differentially skilled at using. As writers we must not be trapped into thinking that they are any more than cultural conventions.

The dividing line between fact and fiction thus becomes blurred in the auto-biographical and biographical text, for if an author can make up facts about his or her life, who is to know what is true and what is false? The point is, however, as Sartre notes, that if an author thinks something existed and believes in its existence, its effects are real.[8] Since all writing is fictional, made up out of things that could have happened or did happen, it is necessary to do away with the distinction between fact and fiction.

To Summarize

Figure 1.1 summarizes the concepts and terms that have historically defined the (auto)biographical method. They provide a road map for the chapters that follow.

Term/Method	Key Features	Forms/Variations
Method	A way of knowing	Subjective, objective
Life	Period of existence; lived experiences	Partial, complete, edited, public, private
Self	Ideas, images, and thoughts of self	Self-stories, autobiographies
Experience	Confronting and passing through events; meanings are constructed	Problematic, routine, ritual
Epiphany	Moment of revelation in a life	Major, minor, relived, illuminative
Autobiography	Personal history of one's life	Complete, edited, topical
Ethnography	Written account of a culture or group	Realist, interpretive, descriptive

(Continued)

(Continued)

Term/Method	Key Features	Forms/Variations
Autoethnography	Account of one's life as an ethnographer	Complete, edited, partial
Biography	History of a life	Autobiography
Story	A fiction, narrative	First or third person
Fiction	An account, something made up, fashioned	Story (life, self)
History	Account of how something happened	Personal, oral, case
Discourse	Telling a story, talking about a text, a text	First or third person
Narrator	Teller of a story	First or third person
Narrative	A story, having a plot and existence separate from the life of the teller	Fiction, epic, science, folklore, myth
Writing	Inscribing, creating a written text	Logocentric, deconstructive
Difference	Every word carries traces of another word	Writing, speech
Personal history	Reconstruction of life based on interviews and conversations	Life history, life story
Oral history	Personal recollections of events, their causes and effects	Work, ethnic, religious, personal, musical, etc.
Case history	History of an event or social process, not of a person	Single, multiple, medical, legal
Life history	Account of a life based on interviews and conversations	Personal, edited, topical, complete
Life story	A person's story of his or her life, or a part thereof	Edited, complete, topical, fictional

Term/Method	Key Features	Forms/Variations
Self story	Story of self in relation to an event	Personal experience, fictional, true
Personal experience story	Story about personal experience	Single, multiple, episode, private, or communal folklore
Case study	Analysis and record of single case	Single, multiple

Figure 1.1 Terms/Forms and Varieties of the (Auto)Biographical Method

Now for a genealogy of terms, the topic of the next chapter.

Notes

1. Where one opens up this history is somewhat arbitrary. See Schutz (1932/1967, p. 5) for a review; also Simmel (1909/1950). Clearly, W. I. Thomas and Florian Znaniecki's (1918–1920) multivolume work *The Polish Peasant in Europe and America* is part of this early concern for the subject and his or her subjective life experiences (Wiley, 1986). William James (1890/1950) and the other American pragmatists Dewey, Peirce, and Mead, also participated in this early focus on the individual and his or her presence in the world.

2. The autobiography, the root form of the biography, has been a central preoccupation of Western literature and the discourse of modernism at least since Augustine (AD 354–430) wrote his *Confessions*. See Elbaz (1987, pp. vii, 18), but also see Misch (1951, ch. 2) for a discussion of the earlier origins of the autobiography as a literary form or genre in the ancient civilizations of the Middle East. The metaphysics of presence, coupled with the concept of a self who can write its history, has been "continuous throughout the ages" (Elbaz, 1987, p. vii; see also Foucault, 1980; Derrida, 1967/1973). On hermeneutics, see Heidegger (1962) and Gadamer (1976). Also see Plummer (1983, ch. 2) for a review of the history of this method in sociology. The term *pathography* has been recently coined to describe those culturally based, popular autobiographies that draw upon a member's condition, or pathology, like alcoholism, mental illness, child abuse, or sexual violence. With this word, like its television counterpart, *docudrama*, a story is reduced to a category which has a ready-made readership in the larger marketplace of cultural consumers.

3. I am indebted to Norbert Wiley for calling this Ricoeur manuscript to my attention.

4. See Peterson (1986, pp. 9, 121). Peterson also notes that this concept is present in the Old Testament.

5. See Kohli (1981, pp. 69–72) for a review.

6. However, see Elbaz (1987, pp. 9–13).

7. See Elbaz (1987, p. 13) and the discussion of obituaries in Chapter 6.

8. See also Thomas and Thomas (1928, pp. 571–572).

2

A Clarification of Terms

What Is Autoethnography?[1]

Deborah E. Reed-Danahay (1997):

> Autoethnography is a form of self-narrative that places the self within a social context. It is both a method and a text. (p. 6)

Tami Spry (2001):

> Autoethnography is...a self-narrative that critiques the situatedness of self and others in social context. (p. 710; see also Alexander, 2000)

Carolyn Ellis (2009):

> As an autoethnographer, I am both the author and focus of the story, the one who tells and the one who experiences, the observer and the observed.... I am the person at the intersection of the personal and the cultural, thinking and observing as an ethnographer and writing and describing as a storyteller. (p. 13)

Mark Neumann (1996):

> Autoethnographic texts...democratize the representational sphere of culture by locating the particular experiences of individuals in tension with dominant expressions of discursive power. (p. 189)

Leon Anderson (2006):

> Analytic autoethnography has five key features. It is ethnographic work in which the researcher (a) is a full member in a research group or setting; (b) uses analytic reflexivity; (c) has a visible narrative presence in the written text; (c) engages in dialogue with informants beyond the self; (d) is committed to an analytic research agenda focused on improving theoretical understandings of broader social phenomena. (p. 374)

Stacy Holman Jones (2005):

Autoethnography is a blurred genre...a response to the call.... [I]t is setting a
scene, telling a story, weaving intricate connections between life and art...making
a text present...refusing categorization...believing that words matter and writing
toward the moment when the point of creating autoethnographic texts is to change
the world. (p. 765)

Finally, Stacy Holman Jones, Tony Adams, and Carolyn Ellis (2013a,
paraphrase):

Autoethnography is the use of personal experience and personal writing to (1) pur-
posefully comment on/critique cultural practices; (2) make contributions to existing
research; (3) embrace vulnerability with purpose; and (4) create a reciprocal relationship with audiences in order to compel a response.

Apples and oranges—are these different tasks or different sides of the
same coin? Mills (quoted in the Preface) and Jones want to rewrite history.
Anderson wants to improve autoethnography by using analytic reflexivity.
Ellis wants to embed the personal in the social. Spry's (2011) self-narratives
critique the social situatedness of identity (see also Adams, 2011). Neumann
(1996) wants to "democratize the representational sphere of culture" by writing outward from the self to the social (p. 186). Jones et al. (2013a) want to
move audiences to action. So do I.

Sartre (1971/1981) reminds us:

No individual is just an individual; each person is a *universal singular,* summed
up and for this reason universalized by his or her historical epoch, each person
in turn reproducing himself or herself in its singularity. Universal by the singular
universality of human history, singular by universalizing singularity in his or her
projects, the person requires simultaneous examination from both ends. (p. ix–x,
paraphrase)

A Genealogy of Terms

Consider the following terms. They all circulate in the present:

1. *Performance* (Conquergood, 1985): to enact: mimesis (imitation),
poiesis (construction), kinesis (resistance) as transgressive accomplishment;
an act of intervention or resistance; dialogic, as experience, as performance
of possibilities, as deconstruction, as ethical mandate (Madison, 2005, pp.
150–179; 2012, pp. 166–208).

Monday's Body (Goodall, 2012, pp. 724–725)

Toward the end of my last chemo cycle, I composed a poem to capture what my body was experiencing:

I have numb Monday fingers, a chemo side effect known as

Neuropathy. Can't touch cold items without pain . . .

Blame my mouth. Chemo mouth, Chemo tongue . . .

Coffee is still good.

Imagine that you are me. full-bodied me,

post chemo-treatment me . . .

On Monday I become forgetful . . .

I drop nouns . . . My nose runs . . .

I think this poem is the body spelled out in

Entropy . . . The body—my body—is losing

life one letter at a time.

And I know I am slowly dying.

And in these words—painful, sad, poetic—Goodall writes his way into death.

2. *Performance:* to study persons as if they were performers, or to study performers; an interpretive event; dialogical performance as ethical imperative; performance ethnography as the doing of critical theory (Conquergood, 1985; Madison, 2012).

Tami Spry (2013; sitting in a wooden chair, hands grasping the back of a chair in front of her, rocking back and forth, as if she were riding a horse):

When I was a girl, I wanted a horse. At four I told people I wanted to be a horseback rider when I grew up. . . . I pictured myself looking something like Sharon Stone in *The Quick and the Dead.* That's what I wanted to be. I rode Western where you hold reins with one hand and grip with your legs because sometimes it's a bumpy ride. (p. 482)

3. *Performance (performative) writing*: writing that shows, does not tell, hesitates, stutters, enacts what it describes, is evocative, reflexive; writing to embrace, enact, embody, effect (Madison, 2012, pp. 220–232).

The Wire

Once I held a blade—sharp and even, slender and perfect in its capacity—over my skin. The veins under my freckled pale skin are like my father's. . . . Once I held a blade over a deep blue vein in my arm. . . . The blade would have let my blood pour, to flood like a Montana river in early spring. (Halley, 2012, p. 19)

This is performance writing; Halley's text performs its own story, as does Spry's (above).

4. *Performativity/performative I:* the speaking subject is constituted for, by, and in language (Pollock, 1998a, p. 9); the reflexive self performing itself (Spry, 2011, p. 30).

Once I held the blade over a deep blue vein in my arm.

5. *Ethnography* (Clifford & Marcus, 1986): inscribing culture, writing culture versus performing culture; **types:** realist, confessional, dramatic, critical, auto (Van Maanen, 2011).

Once I held the blade over a deep blue vein in my arm.

6. *Autoethnography:* reflexively writing the self into and through the ethnographic text; isolating that space where memory, history, performance, and meaning intersect; **types** *(form)*: poetic (Hanauer, 2012); critical reflexive (Madison, 2012, pp. 197–199), analytic, evocative, narrative, performative, collaborative, political, postcolonial, transnational, relational; *(content)*: family, place, other, trauma (loss, illness, abuse, sexuality, race, death, divorce), embodied, queer (see Jones et al., 2013a).

A Holocaust memory, a poetic autoethnography. David Hanauer (2012) is a second-generation holocaust survivor. In 1939, his father, who was a 10-year-old child, was sent by his parents from Germany on one of the limited number of transportations of Jewish-German children to England known as Kindertransport. His father's parents were murdered by the Nazis. Hanauer has been writing his way through this experience, the guilt of being a second-generation Holocaust survivor: He offers a poetic autoethnography as testimony to these events and experiences:

There is no death

as death in a concentration camp:

a faceless burning of distorted

imageless corpses. A death in which

no one cares, no one feels and

everything is in abstract. A

death that is completely impersonal,

detached and distant. A death

empty, all consuming that leaves

you nothing to clutch, nothing to hold

but a hollow memory. (p. 848)

7. *Autoethnography as disruptive practice:* inclusive, political, utopian.

Once I held the blade over a deep blue vein in my arm.

8. *Ethnodrama* (Saldana, 2005, 2011): monologues, monologues with dialogue and ethnodramatic extensions, often involving the audience in post-performance feedback.

9. *Duoethnography* (Norris & Sawyer, 2012): a collaborative research methodology in which two or more researchers juxtapose their life histories in order to provide multiple understandings of a social phenomenon (Norris & Sawyer, 2012, pp. 9–10). Duoethnographers use their own biographies as sites of inquiry and engage in dialogic narrative, often realized in collaborative writing and collaborative autoethnography (see Gale, Pelias, Russell, Spry, & Wyatt, 2013).

10. *Collaborative writing,* collaborative autoethnography (Diversi & Moreira, 2009; Gale & Wyatt, 2009; Wyatt, Gale, Gannon, & Davies, 2011): the coproduction of an autoethnographic (duoethnography) text by two or more writers, often separated by time and distance.

On Why We Wrote Together

This book is about our dialogic collaboration.... Instead of writing alone, each with his own book, we decided to bring our research and writings together in an attempt to instantiate our call for collaborative production of knowledge.... This type of writing exemplifies the very connectedness and co-construction of meaning that we advocate in any type of social science preoccupied with empowering praxis. (Diversi & Moreira, 2009, p. 28)

11. *Collective biography* (Davies & Gannon, 2006; Wyatt et al., 2011): a coproduced, intertwined, reflexive biography, working with memory and storytelling. It begins with storytellers in a group listening and questioning each other concerning their earliest memories in relation to the chosen topic. A cycle of talking, listening, writing, and rewriting continues until everyone is satisfied. Collective biography is done as collaborative writing (Wyatt et al., 2011):

Jonathan (as narrator):	The four of us have written together since last...summer, exchanging writings across the ether...Ken and me in UK and Bronwyn and Sue in...Out of these tangled lines we have fashioned a play in 4 acts. (p. 25)
Deleuze:	One's always writing to bring something to life, to free life from where it's trapped, to trace lines of flight. (p. 37)
Bronwyn:	What collective biography does...is to clear a space for speaking and listening and writing....I love that in our writing we invoke precisely this—the time of day, the wind, the heat, the excruciating pain and pleasure of becoming in that moment (pp. 38, 40)....Collaborative writing is...dangerous...is to be co-implicated with the other to be present to be assailed by thoughts...to be singular to exist in the space of writing with. (pp. 130–131)

To do collective biography is to be vulnerable to the other, to be willing to move through a space that is simultaneously collaborative, autoethnographic, and reflexive (Chang, Ngunjiri, & Hernandez, 2013, p. 17).

12. *Group storytelling*: A variation on the collective biography is the method of having subjects in groups develop their own versions of their life histories. McCall (1985, 1989) created storytelling groups of persons born in the 1940s. She met with these groups weekly over a several-month period. Group participants were given assignments to write stories about a variety of different topics or events in their lives, including their marriages, their work, their divorces, their first dates, the birth of their children, and so on. A recurring theme of the stories dealt with the changing American family and the place of these individuals, as single parents, in this institution.

Jean Richards, married in 1961 and divorced in 1974, comments on the problems in her life:

Ending a marriage and beginning an education, I literally bit off more than I could chew. I lost weight, developed ulcers, became temperamental.... I asked all the questions.... How would I make the house payments? Where would I get the money for food and clothes?... What about Christmas? Who can I turn to? (quoted in McCall & Wittner, 1988, p. 13)

McCall and Wittner (1988) observe that, "reading their stories aloud and discussing them, members of these storytelling groups also created new shared understandings of their lives and their life problems they shared" (p. 14). Their research shows how ordinary people "create culture when they tell stories" (p. 14). The selves of these ordinary people become consubstantial with the stories they told one another. Not only did they create culture, but they created and recreated themselves in the process.

13. *Deconstructive (auto)ethnography* (Jackson & Mazzei, 2009, 307–313): shifts attention from the narrative I to the performative I, contesting the meanings given to voice, presence, experience, and subjectivity.

14. *Critical performance (auto)ethnography*: Conquergood's triad of triads: (1) the I's: imagination, inquiry, intervention; (2) the A's: artistry, analysis, activism; (3) the C's: creativity; citizenship, civic struggles for social justice (Madison, 2005, p. 171; 2012, pp. 189–190).

Divorce: The Aftermath

The man in the crevice knows I will never love again. He... watches as I walk the beach below him and he cackles with crazed insight.... A screamer lives across from me. During the winter her anguish is silent but come the warmth she broadcasts to the neighborhood: "You make me so goddamned sick. I can't stand it anymore." ... We who know the importance of the spectacle live here in Rogers Park, Chicago's last stand before acquiescing to the north shore suburbs. The Eleanor Rigby's of the world find their way here.... Two weeks ago a 16-year-old boy was shot to death in the park in front of the el tracks.... Tonight I visited the park for the first time since the crime. The lawn has been reseeded and in between the plastic City of Chicago garbage cans, the struggling lilac trees send skyward their elegiac bloom. (Gorman, 2012, pp. 843–440)

Gorman's words perform Conquergood's triad. She writes from her postdivorce space; walking the cold, windy shores of Lake Michigan, she finds hope with the Eleanor Rigbys of the world, the man in the crevice, the woman who howls, the murdered 16-year-old boy.

15. *Performance (auto)ethnography* (Denzin, 2003; Pelias, 2011): the merger of critical pedagogy, performance ethnography, and cultural politics; the creation of texts that move from epiphanies to the sting of memory, the personal to the political, the autobiographical to the cultural, the local to the historical. A response to the successive crises of democracy and capitalism that shape daily life; showing how these formations repressively enter into and shape the stories and performances persons share with one another. It shows how persons bring dignity and meaning to their lives in and through these performances; it offers kernels of utopian hope of how things might be different, better. Consider this excerpt from Madison (2010), which describes her purposes in her book *Acts of Activism*:

Performance, Activism and Social Justice

The focus of this book is to address the relationship between performance and local activism in the service of human rights and social justice.... I have witnessed courageous interventions by men and woman who have faced great risks in the defense of human rights and social justice. I have also witnessed how they employ performance as a means of communication and as a subversive tactic to win hearts and minds in their efforts toward a more human and humane society. (p. 1)

In the Beginning

In the beginning there was *biography*, and autobiography, writers writing about writers, writers writing about themselves. Some of these writers wrote ethnographies, accounts about the ways of life of the writer and those written about. Eventually *ethnography* referred to an inscriptive practice captured in the phrase *writing culture* (Clifford & Marcus, 1986). Under the writing culture framework the "culture of a people is seen as an ensemble of texts . . . which the anthropologists struggle to read over the shoulders of those to whom they properly belong" (Geertz, 1973, p. 452; Clifford & Marcus, 1986). Then there was *performance*, the understanding that people (writers) perform culture, through their interpretive (writing) practices (Conquergood, 1985).

Performance throws the "ethnocentrism of the textual model into stark relief when applied to slave culture and other disenfranchised people forcibly excluded from acquiring literacy" (Conquergood, 1998, p. 28). Instead of an "ensemble of texts, a repertoire of performance practices became the backbone of this counterculture where politics was played, danced and acted, as well as sung and sung about . . . because words were never enough to communicate the unsayable" (Gilroy, 1991, p. 37).

The turn to performance argues that we should study persons as performers and cultures as performative or ethnodramatic accomplishments (Saldana, 2011). The goal always is to create the conditions for a critical consciousness, one that imagines a radical politics of possibility. *Autoethnography* inserted itself in the picture when it was understood that all ethnographers reflexively (or unreflexively) write themselves into their ethnographies. The ethnographer's writing self **cannot not** be present, there is **no** objective space outside the text. This is the space of critical performance (auto)ethnography; the space of Conquergood's triad of triads; the intersection of imagination, activism, and civic struggle; the space of Madison's performative acts of activism.

Writing Together–Duoethnography: A Dialogical Space

Terms flow together, intermingle, a montage of overlapping projects, images, voices, techniques. Duoethnography, collaborative autoethnography, collective biography, and *collaborative writing*—alone, together, voices seeking a home. Two or more persons writing together move Madison's acts of activism into a liminal dialogical space. Duoethnographers merge their writing selves, into a multivoiced performance text (Gale et al., 2013, p. 165). The writing surges and flows, a to-ing and fro-ing, fingers poised over keys, eyes on screens, writers writing back and forth, coproducing performance narratives, collective biographies, telling (and writing) intersecting life stories, doing co-performances, laughing and joking, hugging, crying (Gale et al., 2013, p. 166; Davies & Gannon, 2006; Norris & Sawyer, 2012).

Betweener Talk

We can't press the keys at the same time. But this introduction and the entire book are ours. Equally ours. Even as I type this sentence, 2000 miles away from my writing partner I know that these words, meanings, intentions, and emotions reside not in me but in us. . . . After a few attempts at keeping the story straight, we gave in and embraced the exhilarating experience of co-constructing a book together. (Diversi & Moreira, 2009, p. 13)

Definitions: one long word, no hyphens: duoethographycollaborativeautoethnographycollectivebiographcollaborativewriting.

A family of terms slip and slide, fall over one another: critical embodied, transformative, dialogic, reflexive, participatory, emancipatory, narratives of resistance, plateaus, planes of composition, Deleuze, Guattari, assemblages, affect, nomadic inquiry, rhizomatic, love, loss, praxis writing as a way of being in the world.

Writing together, autoethnographers (duoethnographers) create a shared performance space potentially framed around acts of activism and resistance. Writers write themselves into each other's life, sharing identities, coproducing a critical consciousness, imagining new politics of possibility Readers are invited to think and talk their way into the performance, to enter the conversation, to challenge, contest, create a dialogue (Norris & Sawyer, 2012, pp. 10–11).

Guidelines: Duoethnography, like autoethnography, has its own principles and guidelines (Norris & Sawyer, 2012, pp. 10–11). Norris and Sawyer start with Pinar's (1975, pp. 400–401) concept of *currere*—studying a person's life as a journey. The method of currere, like Sartre's regressive-progressive method, works from the past to the present, moving back and forth in time, unraveling and interpreting a life as it makes itself visible as a universal singular. In this case there are two (or more) lives, moving forward and backward.

Duoethnographies, like reflexive autoethnographies, are disruptive, emergent, dialogic, transformative narratives. They are truthful fictions, critiquing the relationship between the personal, the political, and the historical.

They embody a communitarian ethics of care, a relational ethics that values mutual respect, dignity, and connectedness, a world-making ethic that begins with the self in relation with others (Ellis, 2009, p. 308; Wyatt et al., 2011, p. 109). Clearly this discourse is not standing still. Writing selves are performing new writing practices, blurring fact and fiction, challenging the dividing line between biography, history, writing, autobiography, memory, performer, performed, observer, and observed.

Epiphanies

The subject matter of interpretive autoethnographic research is meaningful biographical experience (Pelias, 2011; Tamas, 2011). Interpretive studies are organized in terms of a biographically meaningful event or moment in a subject's life (Poulos, 2008; Ulmer, 1989). This event, the epiphany (also see Chapter 4), how it is experienced, how it is defined, and how it is woven through the multiple strands of a person's life, constitutes the focus of critical interpretive inquiry (Denzin, 2001).

The biographical project begins with personal history, with the sting of childhood memory, with an event that lingers and remains in the person's life story (Ulmer, 1989, p. 209). This is the space where biography intersects with history, politics, and culture. Autoethnography re-tells and re-performs these life experiences as they intersect in these sites. The life story becomes an invention, a re-presentation, an historical object often ripped or torn out of its contexts and recontextualized in the spaces and understandings of the story.

In writing an autoethnographic life story, I create the conditions for rediscovering the meanings of a past sequence of events (Ulmer, 1989, p. 211). In so doing, I create new ways of performing and experiencing the past. To represent the past this way does not mean to "recognize it 'the way it really was.' It means to seize hold of a memory as it flashes up at a moment of danger" (Benjamin, 1968, p. 257), to see and rediscover the past not as a succession of events, but as a series of scenes, inventions, emotions, images, and stories (Ulmer, 1989, p. 112).

And the same observations hold for collaborative writing, collaborative autoethnography, and duoethnography. As writers enter into one another's writing space, they create the conditions for discovering new meanings and new understandings. In bringing the past into the autobiographical present, I insert myself into the past and create the conditions for rewriting and hence re-experiencing it.

History becomes a montage, moments quoted out of context, "juxtaposed fragments from widely dispersed places and times" (Ulmer, 1989, p. 112). Thus are revealed hidden features of the present as well as of the past. I want to invent a new version of the past, a new history. This is what interpretive autoethnography does.

Here is an example, an excerpt from an ongoing project (Denzin, 2005, 2008, 2011, 2013b).

SCENE ONE: The past: Docile Indians

Voice 1:   Narrator-as-young-boy: When I was little, in the 1940s, living in south central Iowa, my grandmother would tell stories about Indians. She loved to tell the story about the day a tall Indian brave with braided hair came to her mother's kitchen door and asked for some bread to eat. This happened when Grandma was a little girl, probably around 1915.

Voice 2:   Grandmother: This Indian was so polite and handsome. Mother said his wife and children stood right behind him in a straight row. The Indian said his name was Mr. Thomas. He was a member of the Fox Indian Nation. He said that he and his wife and his children were traveling to the Mesquaki Reservation near Tama, Iowa, to visit relatives. Mother believed him. He said that they had run out of money and did not like to ask for hand-outs, but this looked like a friendly farm house. Mother said it is a crime in this country to be hungry! I believe that, too!

Voice 3:   Grandmother-as-young-daughter: Mother made lunch for Mr. Thomas and his family. They sat under the big oak tree in the front yard and had a picnic. Later, when they were leaving, Mr. Thomas came back to the kitchen and thanked Mother again. He gave her a small handwoven wicker basket as a gift. I treasure to this day this basket. It has become a family heirloom.

SCENE TWO: Real Indians

Voice 4:   Narrator-as-young-boy: When I was not yet ten one Sunday Mother and Dad took my brother and me to Tama, to the Mesquaki Fox Indian Reservation, to see a Pow Wow. I wondered if we'd see Mr. Thomas, if I would even recognize him if he was there. We walked through the mud, past teepees to the center of a big field. Indians in ceremonial dress with paint on their faces and long braids of hair were singing and danc-ing. Some were drumming and singing. At the edge of the field tables under canvas tents were set up. Dad bought some Indian fry bread for all of us, and bottles of cold root beer. We took the fry bread and pop back to the dance area and watched the dancers. Then it rained and the dancing stopped, and we got in the car and drove home.

SCENE THREE: Made-for-movie Indians

Voice 5: **Narrator-as-young-boy**: The next time I saw an Indian was the following Saturday night when grandpa took me to a movie at the Strand Theater in Iowa City. We watched *Broken Arrow* with Jay Silverheels, Jimmy Stewart, Debra Paget, Will Geer and Jeff Chandler, who played Chief Cochise. Those Indians did not look like the Indians on the Tama Reservation. The Tama Indians were less real. They kind of looked like everybody else, except for the dancers in their ceremonial dress.

Process and Performance

The emphasis on self, biography, history, and experience must always work back and forth between three concerns: the concerns of performance, of process, and/or of analysis. A focus on performance produces performance texts, the tale and the telling, like the narrative above. A focus on process examines a social form, or event, for example epiphanies. A focus on analysis looks at the specific lives of individuals who live the process that is being studied in order to locate their lives in their historical moment.

Building on Pollock (2009), Madison (2012), and Thompson (1978), interpretive, biographical materials may be presented in four different ways. First, complex, multileveled performance texts may be written, staged, and performed, for example, the performance narratives assembled by Pelias (2004, 2011).

Second, following Spry (2006, 2011), single personal experience narratives may be presented and connected to the life story of a given individual. Spry (2006) writes that after she lost her son in childbirth,

> things fell apart. The shadowlands of grief became my unwanted field of study.... After losing our son in childbirth, writing felt like the identification of body parts, as if each described piece of the experience were a cumbersome limb that I could snap off my body and lay upon the ground. (pp. 340–341)

Third, a collection of self and personal experience stories may be collected and grouped around a common theme. Stewart (2005) does this in her essay on cultural poiesis. She records and performs episodes from mundane, everyday

life, including making trips to daycare, the grocery store, and picking up the
sick dog at the vet:

> My story, then, is not an exercise in representation.... Rather it is a cabinet of curios-
> ities designed to excite curiosity. (p. 1040)

Davies and Gannon (2006) describe their collaborative biography project:

> Throughout these chapters we write and reflect on moments of being, on the ambivalent,
> slippery subject-in-process—as infant, schoolgirl, writer, teacher, professor, student, lover,
> wife, daughter/mother—captured in the remembered *moment of being*, transformed
> in a process of telling and writing and reading that *moves* us in a variety of ways.
> These moments and movements are not towards the transformation of ourselves into
> new subjects in linear time. Rather, the transformation lies in a particular form of
> attention to, the remembered moment, an attention that makes the subject's vulner-
> ability to discursive power starkly visible while making visible the constitutive powers
> of the subject-in-process (p. x, italics in original).

Fourth, the researcher can offer a cross-case analysis of the materials that have been collected, paying more attention to the process being
studied than to the persons whose lives are embedded in those processes.
Glaser and Strauss (1967) did this in their classic analysis of the awareness
contexts (open, closed, suspicion, pretense) that surround death and dying
in the modern hospital.

Davies (2006, pp. 185–186) speaks of the stories collected in Davies and
Gannon (2006):

> Each of the stories we have gathered here ... had for us, in the Moment of telling
> them, writing them and listening to them had a breath-stopping, heart-stopping
> quality that made us weep for the feeling of trueness, or being there.... Collective
> biography works best with early stories, since that is when we had the clearest access
> of being present in the moment.

Collective biography is about writers being present in the moment, writing
from the soul, constructing a space where selves flow together, being vulnerable, pushing always for connections between personal troubles and public
issues. Here in the moment of the present, writers interrogate that space where
praxis intersects with pedagogy. Here in the now of the present a radical politics of possibility is made visible.

It is recommended that interpretive autoethnographic studies be sensitive to
each of the above modes of presentation. Because any individual can tell multiple

stories about his or her life, it must be understood that a life will consist of multiple narratives. No self or personal experience story will encompass all of the stories that can—or could—be told about a single life, nor will any personal history contain all of the self stories that could be told about that life's story. Multiple narratives, drawn from the self stories of many individuals located in different points in the process being interpreted can be secured. This triangulation, or combination of biographical methods, ensures that performance, process, analysis, history, and structure receive fair and thorough consideration in any inquiry. The interpreter always works outward from the epiphany to those sites where memory, history, structure, and performance intersect, the spaces of Tami Spry's (2006, p. 340) performative I (see also Madison, 2012). These are performances that interrupt and critique hegemonic structures of meaning (Spry, 2011, p. 35).

The Sting of Memory

By revisiting the past through remembered experiences, I insert myself in my family's history with Native Americans. This history is part of a deeper set of mid-century memories about Indians, reservations, life on the Midwest plains, and American culture. As I narrate these experiences, I begin to understand that I, along with my family, am a participant in this discourse. I am a player in a larger drama, performing the parts culture gives to young White males. From the vantage of the present I can look back with a critical eye on those family performances, but the fact of my participation in them remains. We turned Native Americans into exotic cultural objects. We helped them perform nonthreatening versions of Indian-ness, versions that conformed to those tame Indians I watched on the silver screen.

A *mystory* text begins with those moments that define a crisis, a turning point in the person's life. Ulmer (1989) suggests the following starting point:

> Write a mystory bringing into relation your experience with three levels of discourse—personal (autobiography), popular (community stories, oral history or popular culture), [and] expert (disciplines of knowledge). In each case use the punctum or sting of memory to locate items significant to you. (p. 209)

The sting of memory locates the moment, the beginning. Once located this moment is dramatically described, fashioned into a text to be performed. This moment is then surrounded by those cultural representations and voices that define the experience in question. These representations are contested, challenged.

The sting of the past. A string of childhood and young adulthood memories: My brother and I are watching *The Lone Ranger*. We are playing cowboys and Indians—I'm Tonto. Thanksgiving, fourth grade, Coralville, Iowa:

I'm dressed up as Squanto in the Thanksgiving play; my grandparents are in the audience. Summer 1960: I'm older now, drinking and driving fast down country roads, playing loud country music. I'm a cowboy now, not an Indian. I fall in love with June Carter singing "Ring of Fire." Wedding, Winter 1963: I close my eyes and remember Sunday fish fries along the Iowa River, hayrides and football on Friday night, homecoming dances in the University High School gym, pretty girls in blue sweaters and white bobby socks, tall young men with blue suede shoes, flat top haircuts, Elvis singing "Heart Break Hotel."

I wish I could reach back and hold on to all of this, things I loved then. James Lee Burke (2009) reminds me that the secret is "to hold on to the things you loved, and never give them up for any reason" (p. 274). But did I really love them or was I just afraid to act like I didn't love them? Which self was I performing? Have I really talked myself into giving them up?[2]

I've always been performing, even in front of the black-and-white TV. The dividing line between person and character, performer and actor, stage and setting, script and text, performance and reality has disappeared, if it ever existed. For a moment I was Tonto, and then I was Squanto. Illusion and make-believe prevail; we are who we are through our performative acts. Nothing more, nothing less.

Conclusions

Terms and assumptions have been defined. The many different ways of writing and performing autoethnography have been discussed. The next chapter takes up the topics of selves, stories, voice, and experience.

Notes

1. Materials in this section draw from Denzin (2013b). Minge and Zimmerman (2013, pp. 12–13) state, "today, autoethnography encompasses a multitude of terms and writing forms such as Crawford's personal ethnography, Ellis and Bochner's reflexive ethnography, Ellis's emotional sociology, Wolcott's ethnographic autobiography, Ronai-Rambo's layered account, Denzin's experiential texts, and Reed-Danahay's autobiographical ethnography (see Adams, Jones, & Ellis, 2013; Ellis, 2013; Jones, Adams, & Ellis, 2013a).

2. This paragraph steals from Burke (2009, p. 274).

3

Interpretive Guidelines

Jann S. Wenner (to Bob Dylan):	I've gone through all of the collected articles that have appeared, all the early ones and Columbia Records' biographies, that's got the story about running away from home at 11 and 12 and 13-and-a-half. . . . Why did you put out that story?
Bob Dylan:	I didn't put out any of those stories.
Jann S. Wenner:	Well, it's the standard Bob Dylan biography.
Bob Dylan:	Well, you know how it is. If you're sittin' in a room, and you have to have something done. . . . I was playing at Town Hall, and the producer of it came over with that biography. I'm a songwriter, I'm not a biography writer. . . . So I'm sitting in a room with some people, and I say, "Come on now, I need some help; gimme a biography," so there might be three or four people there and out of those three or four people maybe they'll come up with something, come up with a biography. So we put it down, it reads well and the producer gets a kick out of it. . . . But in actuality, this thing wasn't written for hundreds thousands of people . . . it was just for whoever was going in there and getting a ticket, you know, they get one of these things too. That's just show business. (Wenner, 2013, p. 17)

Selves and lives are storied performances. Sometime these stories and the selves they tell about are collaborative productions, as when three or four people sat around and made up a story about Bob Dylan's early childhood.

In earlier chapters, I defined the autobiographical/autoethnographic project as the studied use and collection of life documents that describe turning-point moments in an individual's life. It remains to examine how these moments are studied, understanding that we only study the representations of experience. I begin with an extended discussion of lived experience and voice.

Writing About Lived Experience

Narrative texts freeze events and lived experiences into rigid sequences. Indeed, traditional ethnographic writing is structured by a logic that separates writer, text, and subject matter. Any text can be analyzed in terms of four paired terms: (a) the "real" and its representations, (b) the text and its author and presumed reader, (c) lived experience and its textual representations, and (d) the subject and his or her intentional meanings.

In the Dylan story there is the flesh-and-blood Dylan, the songwriter, and performer. Then there is this story about his childhood, which he says was made up; indeed, he disavows any responsibility for the story. He asks the reader to just take it as a story, nothing more.

The ambiguities and complexities of life situations thus seldom appear in the analyst's text. The corpus of experience disappears into a text that is then read as a representation of the life experiences of the individual being studied. In the quote above, where is the real Dylan?[1]

There are no experiences outside the text, only glossed, narrative reports of them. The use and the value of the autoethnographic method lies in its user's ability to capture, probe, and render understandable problematic experience. If this cannot be done, if subject representations of lived experiences, as given in stories, cannot be represented, then the method ends up producing the kinds of documents I have criticized in preceding chapters.

Experience can be studied only through performance (Bruner, 1986, p. 6). The autoethnographer seeks to "extract meaning from experience rather than to depict experience exactly as it was lived" (Bochner, 2000, p. 270; see also Adams & Jones, 2008, p. 374). However, what counts as experience or performance is shaped by a politics of representation, and hence is "neither self-evident nor straight-forward: it is always contested and always therefore political" (Scott, 1993, p. 412), shaped by matters of race, class, gender, sexuality, and age. Representations of experience are performative, symbolic, and material. Anchored in performance events, they include drama, ritual, and storytelling.

The Poststructural Turn

Poststructuralists and autoethnographers who queer autoethnography presume that there is not a real world out there that can be captured by a "knowing" author through careful transcription and analysis of field materials (interviews, field notes, etc.; see Adams & Jones, 2008, p. 379). The writer is no longer regarded as the window to the world under study. Rather, the world and the subject are textual constructions. The flesh-and-blood subject is always translated into either an analytic subject as a social type or a textual subject who speaks from the author's pages.

Several questions follow from this formulation. Who is the subject? Does the subject have direct access to his or her lived experiences? Is there a layer of experience that is authentic and real? Must we always trust what a subject says about the meaning of an experience? Is the subject's word final? Does the literal translation of talk equal lived experiences and its meanings?

The assumptions behind these questions must be challenged. Language and speech do not mirror experience; rather, they create representations of experience. Meanings are always in motion, inclusive, conflicting, contradictory. There are gaps between reality, experience, and performances. There is never pure presence. We have reached the end of pure description. Description becomes inscription, and inscription becomes performance. The task is to understand what textually constructed presence means because there is only the text.

Voice, Presence, Experience

Voice is often taken to be the true measure of presence, that is, "voice simulates . . . presence" (Derrida, 1967/1973, p. 15). Voice, in older paradigms

has frequently been privileged because it has assumed that voice can speak the truth of consciousness and experience. In these paradigms, voice lingers close to the true and the real . . . and is a mirror to the self.

Qualitative researchers have been trained to privilege this voice. (Mazzei & Jackson, 2009, p. 1, paraphrase)

Voice is only one form of presence, and indeed once spoken, the "voice in its presentness . . . vanishes immediately . . . and our poor attempts to capture it on tape or in fieldnotes always fail." (St. Pierre, 2009, p. 222)

Voice "is part of the humanist discursive . . . formation poststructuralism works against (St. Pierre, 2009, p. 221). Transcribed speech cannot just speak for itself (Mazzei & Jackson, 2009, p. 3). Its meanings are not transparent, and the construction of the written text based on speech is just that, a construction.

To hear is to perceive, to be aware of a sound—the sound of the other's voice; to acknowledge, to attend to, to ascertain, to catch, to discover, to eavesdrop, to examine, to heed, to understand, to seek a hearing of one's voice, to be heard. But the speaking subject is never just heard. Everyday natural (not transcribed) talk is visual, theatrical, inflective, rhetorical.

When we speak we "expose" our thoughts as they are put into words. . . . When we speak we want our interlocutor to listen to us; we revive his (her) attention with meaningless interpellations (of the type "Hello"). . . . Unassuming as they are, these words and expressions are . . . discreetly dramatic. (Barthes, 1985, pp. 3–5)

A Deconstructive Autoethnography

Taking a poststructural approach to autoethnography, Jackson and Mazzei (2008, p. 300) deconstruct the researcher as subject "in order to confront the limits of a reliance on experience and narrative voice in the genre." Extending the familiar arguments of Scott (1991, 1992, 1993), Butler (1993), MacLure (2011), and St. Pierre (2009), they question the unproblematic reliance on voice, presence, and experience in much autoethnographic writing. Such a view leads to a focus on the narrative self, the self with an unproblematic window to the past, a self with a clear voice anchored in past experience, a self telling stories worth telling (Ellis & Bochner, 2000; Jackson & Mazzei, 2008, p. 300).

In contrast, a deconstructive autoethnography makes experience, voice, and presence problematic (see below). The performative I puts experience under erasure, showing how experience itself produces the construction of the subject (Jackson & Mazzei, 2008, p. 305). A deconstructive reading of the I in autoethnography de-centers the knowing I, challenges the writer's voice, unsettles the concept of past experiences as the site of subjectivity, and opens the door for multiple voices and perspectives to be heard and performed and seen.

Tami Spry (2011):

I am in the bathroom of a disco, circa 1980.

I am white, 19, 110 pounds, blonde . . .

In this mostly Black disco.

Four Black women

follow me into the bathroom.

Standing in front of the mirror . . .

Which we as our looking glass . . .

To reify Black, White, Pretty, Sexy.

Kate Davy says that "white womanhood

Is a racialization process

played out on many fronts,"

not the least of which positions

the black woman as sexual monster

and the white women as sexually

innocent, pure, and gentile,

authorized by the dictates

of white womanhood. (p. 146, paraphrase)

It's all here: mirrors, racialized selves, fragmented identities, the White gaze, the Black gaze, race and gender in the bathroom, circa 1980. It could have been yesterday.

The unified speaking subject with full access to her thoughts and intentions is a myth. Even though "performance appears to express prior intention, a doer *behind* the deed, the prior agency is only legible as the effect of that utterance" (Butler, 1995, p. 227; see also St. Pierre, 2009, p. 227). Dylan speaks, tells a story, performs, but there is no real Dylan behind these utterances, only another Dylan with another set of stories.

A deconstructive autoethnography problematizes the writer's authority and all-knowing presence in the text. We seek de-authorizing devices (Lather, 2009, p. 22) such as messy tests, shifting counter-voices, voices talking over one or past one another, split texts, stuttering voices, repetitions, silences, mimicry, exaggerations, mischief-making talk that disrupts and disguises itself (MacLure, 2011, pp. 97–98, 2013; Pollock, 1998a). There is an attempt to recover and perform the "open spaces of agency where fractured, transgressive, stubborn historical subjects make their own [inconclusive] histories" (Pollock, 1998a, p. 19, paraphrase).

Sophie Tamas (2011) on the phone:

I am 29 years old, washing dishes in a rented run-down three

bedroom row house on a small Canadian town . . . Dora is drooling beside

me an ExerSaucer. The phone rings. I dry my hands . . .

Hello?

Is Joe there?

It's a woman, around my age.

He's away on business . . .

                               Who's this?
That's rude.

                    His wife. Can I help you?

                          Are you serious? You can't be.
I put my hand on the counter.

I am using my best reasonable voice.

                    I have been for ten years. He lives here . . .
Three days later she calls again.

          Hello?

                          I'm so sorry (she is in tears) . . .

                          He bought me a ring. He sends

                          me money.
I don't remember the rest of the conversation. I am cold . . .

She is crazy, almost hysterical . . . My hands are shaking. He never bought

me a ring. . . . It's not true, I decide. So it isn't . . .

Sophie: Why didn't I leave?

Metasophie: You're . . . a dependent idiot

Sophie: Why am I such a basket-case?

Metasophie: Pathetic.

Ubersophie: You could use some help. (pp. 11, 15, 16, 19, paraphrase)

Although the language is deceptively simple and direct, Tamas produces a complex text with multiple and overlapping voices. It is a text filled with emotion, complexity, confusion, selves reflecting on selves. What does this all mean? Where is the meaning? What meaning can she extract from the telephone call?

There is no simple retelling of lived experience. The poststructural writer juxtaposes voices, temporality, and point of view. Emotion is privileged. Narrative truth is emphasized. Tamas tells herself a lie which she believes. The text creates its view of the world. Language is used self-reflexively. Sophie's private emotions are made public. In emphasizing the personal, a new kind of theorizing occurs. Narratives are filled with biographical and not disciplinary citations.

A minimalist theoretical text is sought, a text unmediated by complex theoretical terms and concepts. The text is meant to speak for itself, a site where the writer carries on a dialogue with herself and with the reader.

The Evidence of Experience

More deeply, Scott (1991, 1992, 1993) and Pollock (1998b, 1998c, 2007, 2009) remind us that lived experience is socially constructed. It does not have an ontological reality independent of language and interaction.[2] That is, persons and their lives and their experiences are constituted through discourse in discursive systems which often overlap and contradict one another. Subjects' accounts of experience, including their stories and performances, cannot be taken ipso facto as true or accurate renderings of the real. Individuals "do not have experience, rather subjects are constituted through experience" (Scott, 1991, p. 779).

We study how experience is constituted, framed, discussed, performed, analyzed, talked about, and interpreted. "To think about experience in this way is to historicize it as well as to historicize the identities it produces" (Scott, 1991, p. 780). To think of experience this way is to interrogate the practices that give these identities the appearance of being real and authentic. Experience, at this level, is already performative, it is "at once already an interpretation, and something that needs to be interpreted" (Scott, 1991, p. 797).

Performance as Experience

Extending Scott's arguments, performance that is the expression of experience cannot be appealed to as uncontestable evidence for the meaning of an experience (Scott, 1991, p. 777). Rather, performances are constitutive of experience. They are the practices that allow for the construction of situated identities in specific sites. They are the embodied co-performatives that actually do something in the world (Conquergood, 1998, p. 32; Hamera, 2011, p. 320). Subjects as performers are constituted in and through their co-performative practices. Together, Dylan and his friends constructed a story about Dylan's life.

These acts relationally connect subjects to others, to their yearnings, desires, fears, fantasies (Hamera. 2011, p. 322; Madison, 2012, p. 186).[3] Performative acts have material and affective effects (Clough, 2007). At the sensory level they are felt and have sounds, specific looks, rhythms, movements, gestures, glances, smells (Hamera, 2011, pp. 318–319).

A performative theory of everyday life experiences "celebrates performance as imitation, construction, and resistance. Conquergood (1998, p. 31) rephrases, endowing performances with the restless energies and subversive powers of mimesis, poiesis, and kinesis. Agency is made visible in performative acts of resistance, as well as in mimesis, when imitation functions as criticism, intervention, or disruption. We move, then, from body, to paper, to stage (Spry, 2011). Embodied performance is the stand-in-for and the site of experience. When fused with a social justice initiatives, these co-performances become vehicles for resisting "regimes of oppressive power" (Madison, 2012, p. 189).

Claudio Moreira:

My job is not making the co-performer agree with me.

My job is to articulate a clear text of my moral position that

contains in itself all the arguments needed to

understand the event.

Showing not telling

The tools to the co-performer to follow the move

The critique of the configuration of class/race/gender in a

specific moment, overtly

creating a dialogic moral

I am not doing pieces that reproduce the struggles of the

white middle class in late-capitalism society

I move to that racialized, gendered space to set up a counter-

hegemonic form of resistance. (Diversi & Moreira, 2009, p. 189)

Marcelo Diversi:

And how do you think your version of autoethnography advances decolonizing production of knowledge in the social sciences at this particular historical moment? (Diversi & Moreira, 2009, p. 189)

Claudio Moreira:

My project works outward to the university and its classrooms, treating these spaces as critical public spheres. My voice, both angry and loving, sees these academic spaces as sites for resistance and empowerment in a performative way. (Diversi & Moreira, 2009, p. 189)

Experience as Performance

This view of experience and the performative makes it difficult to sustain any distinction between "appearances and actualities" (Schechner, 1998, p. 362). Further, if, as Butler (1993, p. 141) reminds us, there are no original performances, then every performance establishes itself performatively as an original, a personal and locally situated production. An extended quote from Goffman (1959) summarizes my position.

The legitimate performances of everyday life are not "acted" or "put on" in the sense that the performer knows in advance just what he [she] is going to do, and does this solely because of the effect it is likely to have. The expressions it is felt he [she] is giving off will be especially "inaccessible" to him [her]... but the incapacity of the ordinary individual to formulate in advance the movements of his [her] eyes and body does not mean that he [she] will not express him [her] self through these devices in a way that is dramatized and pre-formed in his [her] repertoire of actions. In short, we all act better than we know how. (pp. 73–74)

The Biographical Illusion

A life, at one level, refers to the biographical experiences of a named person. A person is a cultural creation. Every culture, for example, has names for different types of persons: male, female, husband, wife, daughter, son, professor, student, and so forth. These names are attached to persons. Persons build biographies and identities around the experiences associated with these names (e.g., old man, young man, divorced woman, only daughter, only son).

These experiences have effects at two levels in a person's life. On the *surface level*, effects are unremarkable, barely felt. They are taken for granted and are nonproblematic, as when a person buys a newspaper at the corner grocery, Effects at the *deep level* cut to the inner core of the person's life and leave indelible marks on him or her. These are the *epiphanies* of a life. Interpretive researchers attempt to secure self and personal experience stories that deal with events—mundane and remarkable—that have effects at the deep level of a person's life.

But what is a life? Is it a *biographical illusion* (Bertaux, 1987; Bourdieu, 1986)? Roos (1987, p. 17) discusses this concept in the following passage, in which he cites Pierre Bourdieu (1986):

The joint interest of the object (the person himself) and subject (the researcher getting the story) of the biography project is to construct a coherent story, with a purpose ... is an illusion ... [for] in reality a biography is almost always a discontinuous story which lacks coherence in itself.

Bourdieu compares a life to a subway line "where the stops have no meanings by themselves, only as parts of a larger structure" (quoted in Roos, 1987, p. 17). Within this framework, the biographical project is an illusion, for any coherence that a life has is imposed by the larger culture, by the researcher, and by the subject's belief that his or her life should have coherence. Such a position is consistent with Bourdieu's general structural position which denies the presence and importance of the subject in both theory and everyday life.

Roos departs from Bourdieu on the following important points.[4] First, there are two logics which organize a life story or life history. The first is the logic of the social field, or the larger society and culture where a life is played out. In this social field, the subject may be positioned as an alienated worker, an unemployed female, or a divorced woman. This field will attach a range of meanings to the individuals who inhabit these positions. It will interpolate, or create a body of subjectivities for them. Second, there is the logic of the personal life of the individual who writes his or her life story. This logic may lead persons to believe that they have no control over their life, that they are worthless, or that they do have control and that they are worth something. These two logics may not overlap or coincide. Bourdieu calls these the external and internal logics of a story. When these two logics intersect, according to Bourdieu, the biographical illusion exists. For example, the divorced, unemployed woman may feel stigmatized and worthless, and her life story will express self feelings.

However, as Roos (1987, p. 17) argues, when these logics do not overlap, it becomes more difficult to sustain the argument that biographical coherence is an illusion. Furthermore, and this is Roos's second point, from whose point of view is the illusion seen? If the subject sees coherence and the researcher doesn't, who is correct? At what moment in time is the illusion established? Bourdieu's arguments concerning biographical coherence are important. A similar argument was made in Chapter 1. However, as argued in Chapter 2 in the discussion of experience and its expression, reading an overlap between two fields of experience (the social and the personal) is difficult and involves an imposition of one interpretive frame (the researcher's) on another. Once again, the sociological subject is turned into an object of sociological theorizing.

The point to make is not whether biographical coherence is an illusion or a reality. Rather, what must be established is how individuals give coherence to their lives when they write or talk self-autobiographies. The sources of this coherence, the narratives that lie behind them, and the larger ideologies that structure them must be uncovered.[5] Bourdieu's general position glosses the complexities of this process.

Making Experience Come Out Right

The anthropologist David W. Plath (1987), in an article titled "Making Experience Come Out Right: Culture as Biography," thickens Bourdieu's illusion by showing how culture and cultural meanings are not external to the life and meanings of the self but constitutive of it. A careful and detailed reading of Montaigne's (1572–1588/1958) essays leads Plath to propose that the autobiographical meanings of the self are fundamentally unstable and realized only through time and temporality. Montaigne's self is "consubstantial" with his writings. He wrote himself into his essays. He says of his writings:

> In modeling this figure upon myself, I have had to fashion and compose myself so often to bring myself out, that the model itself has to some extent grown firm and taken shape. Painting myself for others, I have painted my inward self with colors clearer than my original ones. I have no more made my book than my book has made me—a book consubstantial with its author, concerned with my own self, an integral part of my life. (Montaigne, 1958, p. 504)

Each time Montaigne writes himself into his text, he creates a new picture of who he is. He is who he writes, and who he writes keeps changing. His self is a temporal production. He is not a biographical illusion; he is a biographical production. He is attempting to capture his deep, inner, inward self, understanding that he is more than his words make him out to be. His selfhood, as evidenced in his autobiographical writings, can be understood only as a temporal phenomenon, "and not as a 'structure' individuated and spaced-out from the rest of culture. Culture . . . becomes a window-of-opportunity for the completing of self-projects" (Plath, 1987, p. 1).

In this view, Bourdieu's position can be seen as making culture a structure which creates biographies and selves. Plath's position challenges this interpretation and directs our attention, as indicated above, to how persons create and give meaning to their lives in the autobiographical texts they produce. This temporal process will make the self consubstantial with the artifacts the culture makes available to the person. At the same time, the person may be seen as creating artifacts like autobiographies, which are, for them, consubstantial with who they are.

Making Sense of an Individual's Life I: Sartre and Flaubert

Those interpretive projects which attempt to make sense of the subject's life typically, like Sartre (1971/1981), take a subject's works as the beginning point of inquiry. They then attempt to interpret who the subject is by reading through those productions. It is assumed that the "real" subject will be found in these documents. Discussing Flaubert, Sartre phrases this assumption in the following words: "He is objectified in his books. Anyone will tell you, 'Gustave Flaubert—he's the author of *Madame Bovary*.' What then is the relationship of the man to the work" (p. x). If Flaubert is objectified in his works, Sartre finds a part of himself in Flaubert. He states: "Why Flaubert? In rereading his correspondence . . . I felt I had a score to settle and sought to get to know him better" (p. x).

Sartre's project, then, is an attempt to get to know Flaubert better as he attempts to answer the question, "What can we know about a man?" To know a man, Sartre is led to reread all of Flaubert's works, letters, diaries, autobiographies, letters written to him, and accounts others gave of him. He then organizes his study in terms of the following topics: (1) a problem, (2) the father, (3) the mother, (4) the elder brother, (5) the birth of a younger son, (6) father and son, (7) two ideologies, (8) the imaginary child, (9) from imaginary child to actor, (10) from actor to author, (11) scripta mament, and (12) from poet to artist.

Four assumptions organize Sartre's (1971/1981) attempts to understand Flaubert. The first involves where to begin the study:

Now we must begin. How, and by what means? It doesn't much matter: a corpse is open to all comers. The essential thing is to set out with a problem. The one I have chosen is hardly ever discussed. Let me read this passage from a letter. . . . "It is by the sheer force of work that I am able to silence my innate melancholy. But the old nature often reappears, the old nature that no one knows, the deep, always hidden wound." What is the meaning of this? Can a wound be innate? In any event Flaubert refers us to his prehistory. . . . [W]e must try to understand . . . the origin of the wound that is "always hidden" and dates back to his earliest childhood. That will not, I think, be a bad start. (p. x)

Here Sartre exposes his commitment to the view that all life histories have their origins in early childhood. This is his first assumption. The story must begin with the individual's prehistory. His second assumption argues that in this prehistory there will be an event that indelibly shapes the life of the person. For Flaubert, it is a deep, early wound that involved his late entry into language. Sartre's third assumption is evident in the organization of his two-volume work on Flaubert. As noted above, his choice and ordering of topics take Flaubert from childhood through adulthood. They turn on the influences of, first, the father, then the mother, then siblings, then the relation between the father and the son, then early ventures into being an actor and an author. Sartre sees Flaubert's life unfolding through a series and sequences of stages which double back on one another as Flaubert struggles to discover who he is.

Sartre's (1971/1981) fourth assumption involves the problems of telling when Flaubert is telling the truth about his life. He argues: "When have found that Gustave, whenever he writes in the first person, is insincere. . . . But he gives himself up when he invents" (p. 182). When Flaubert exaggerates, his "fiction permits him to say what he feels . . . lying . . . cheats us by truth" (p. 188). Sartre reads many of Flaubert's so-called factual accounts of his life as inventions, often "curious and deceitful text[s] . . . the rule is strict" (pp. 7, 9). In short, what Flaubert says about his life is not to be trusted. What he writes in his fiction is to be taken as truthful. Thus Sartre assumes that there are facts, facticities, and fictions about Flaubert and his life. There are at least two Flauberts: the man who fabricated events and experiences about his "real" life and the man who wrote himself into his fiction. The real Flaubert is to be found in the fictions he wrote. Sartre locates truth in fiction.

Such a position presumes that the real facts and facticities about a life can be discovered. It assumes the presence in fiction of an intentional author whose real meanings can be ascertained. That Flaubert went to such lengths to disguise himself and to misrepresent his experiences should alert us to the fact that he doubted his own intentionality. Like Montaigne, he sought the consubstantiality of himself in his works, and they were all fictions.

Sartre found the Flaubert he wanted to find by positing a real subject who lurked inside his so-called fictional texts. But this distinction between Flaubert's two texts, his first person accounts and his fictions, cannot be allowed.[7] All of Flaubert's writings were fiction. There were (and are) only multiple versions of his subjectivity.

Making Sense of an Individual's Life II: Alcoholics

I turn now to a brief discussion of a variant on Sartre's approach to making sense of an individual's life. Like Sartre, this variant assumes the existence of a pivotal event in a person's life. It also assumes that this event will be a pivotal meaning structure that organizes the other activities in a person's life. This strategy involves studying how this event comes to occupy a central place in a person's life. It then examines how the meanings of this event change over time. It attempts to anchor the meanings of this event in larger cultural settings, including the mass media, the popular culture, and interacting groups.

I employed this approach in my study of American alcoholics (Denzin, 1987a, 1987b). The pivotal meaning structure for the active alcoholic involves drinking and those social acts that connect the person to alcohol. The pivotal meaning structure for the recovering alcoholic involves not drinking, or abstinence from alcohol. Alcoholics Anonymous (AA) replaces alcohol in the lives of many recovering alcoholics.

The Progressive-Regressive Method

In order to study these meaning structures, I watched the performances and listened to the self stories alcoholics told one another around the A.A. meeting tables. From these stories, I worked back in biographical time to discover how the individual first became a drinker, then an alcoholic drinker, and then a recovering alcoholic who no longer drank. I employed a variant of Sartre's (1963, pp. 85–166) progressive-regressive method which begins with a key event in a subject's live and then works forward and backward from that event. In my study, forward progression began with the individual's participation in A.A. and admission of his or her alcoholism. I listened to these individuals as they began to discuss their past life experiences. I worked backward, identifying how the person got to A.A. in the first place.

I then employed three interpretive strategies adopted from Paul Thompson's (1978) treatment of oral history materials. First, I collected single life-story, life-history narratives involving a select number of "old-timers" in the A.A. groups I studied. Second, I collected self stories organized around single themes, like relapses, treatment experiences, marriages and divorces, first getting to A.A., and so on. Third, from these materials, I build an interpretive account of how individuals performed long-term sobriety as A.A. members.

My intentions were not to unravel lives, find the real meanings of lives, or discover who the "real" alcoholic was. Rather, I examined how alcoholics represented themselves to one another in the A.A. setting through the stories they told one another. I assumed, however, that uncovering the meanings to the pivotal event in their lives was a key to understanding how they became recovering alcoholics. In these senses, I stayed within the framework of Sartre's project but departed from it because I made no attempt to probe the prehistory of the A.A. members. Nor did I attempt to discover the "real" person behind the A.A. stories that were told.

Conclusions

I have troubled key terms, including *lives, truth, experience, presence, performance,* and *voice.* The problems of the biographical illusion and biographical coherence were again taken up. In the next chapter I will discuss problems involved in reading lived experiences and treating these experiences as autoethnographic material. I will focus on epiphanies, or turning-point moments in person's lives.

Notes

1. This question is pursued in the 2007 movie *I'm Not There*, a biographical musical directed by Todd Haynes, based on Dylan's multiple life stories and music.
2. Scott (1991, p. 782) reviews different meanings of experience, including experience as a process that is internal, external, objective, subjective, or constitutive of consciousness.
3. Madison (2012, p. 186) recasts performance ethnography as co-performance ethnography.
4. See also Bertaux's discussion of Bourdieu (1987, pp. 47–50).
5. See Denzin (1987b, pp. 190–193) for a discussion of how this works for recovering alcoholics.
6. This has important parallels with the collective biography project discussed by Davies and Gannon (2006).
7. The writings about the life of the playwright Lillian Hellman provide another illustration of this futile attempt to locate the "true" facts about an author (see Feibleman, 1988; Hellman, 1970, 1973, 1976; Kanfer, 1988; Rollyson, 1988; Wright, 1986). Hellman was called "one of the most adventurous and tough-minded playwrights in the history of American theater" (Jane Fonda), a fraud, an "artist of veneer-deep authenticity" (Mary McCarthy), "a mother, a sister, and a friend" (William Styron), "someone who displayed a high finish of integrity, decency and uprightness" (John Hersey), a woman "who could upstage God" (Peter Feibleman). About her writing, Mary McCarthy stated, "Every word she writes is a lie, including 'and' and 'the'" (quoted in Kanfer, 1988, p. 15). By taking the position that truth and fiction are separate productions, the writings on and about Hellman ignore the fact that all of her statements were fictions. The "true" story of Hellman can never be produced.

4 Selves, Stories, Experiences

> I am concerned with the performance of subversive . . . narratives . . . the performance of possibilities aims to create . . . a . . . space where unjust systems and processes are identified and interrogated. (Madison, 1998, pp. 277, 280)

I begin with a story Bill performed. My topic is reading the traces and evidences of turning-point experiences in a person's life.

Bill's Story

Bill is a 30-year-old white male, an engineer, single, sober 6 years in Alcoholics Anonymous. He is telling a version of his life story to an open A.A. meeting. The focus of such stories is specified in A.A.'s, *Alcoholics Anonymous* (1976, p. 58): "Our stories disclose in a general way what we used to be like, what happened, and what we are like now." The story begins:

My name's Bill and I'm an alcoholic. I became an alcoholic at about the age of 16. I learned to drink when I was a sophomore in high school with my friends. We would steal booze from my parent's liquor cabinet. We started drinking before classes started at school. Later I learned how to buy friends with my parent's booze. I had a girlfriend for 8 years. We used to drink together and mess around. Then I lost her. I started drifting after high school. Everybody did. I became a hippie. It was the thing to do. Went to a commune in Oregon and learned how to catch salmon. Took every drug anybody ever took. Built a cabin in the woods and I guess I found God. Anyway I thought he spoke to me. I came back home and decided to just drink beer. I wasn't working. Every day I would go to Al's Pub at 3:00 p.m. and sit in the same chair. But before I went to the Pub I stopped at the bank, it was right around the corner. I'd cash a check, this was every day, for $7.75. Now there's a story behind this which I don't have time to tell you. But anyway, you see I was afraid to make change at the bar. So with $7.75 I had money for three pitchers of beer ($2.00 apiece), .75 for cigarettes, they hadn't gone up yet, and four quarters to play the juke box. I'd sit there until I got good and drunk and then I'd go home and pass out. This went on for three years. $7.75

every day, same bar stool, same three pitchers of beer, same music on the juke box. It got worse. I started seeing things. I ended up in the mental health clinic. Thirty days. Somebody from A.A. came and saw me. I got out, started going to meetings and still drinking. One night I went to my psychiatrist and he told me to stop drinking. I did. I haven't had a drink since that night. I go to 5 meetings a week. I go to Al-Anon. I'm very close to my family. My life has gotten better. Thank you for letting me talk.

I will come back to this story.

Liminality, Ritual, and the Structure of the Epiphany[1]

Within and through their performances, persons are moral beings, already present in the world, ahead of themselves, occupied and preoccupied, like Bill, with everyday doings and emotional practices (see Denzin, 1984, p. 91). However, the postmodern world stages existential crises. Following Turner (1986b) the autoethnographer gravitates to these narratively structured, liminal, existential spaces in the culture. In these sites ongoing social dramas occur. These dramas have complex temporal rhythms. They are storied events, narratives that rearrange chronology into multiple and differing forms and layers of meaningful experience (Turner, 1986b, p. 35). They are epiphanies.

Epiphanies, as argued in Chapter 2, are interactional moments and experiences which leave marks on people's lives. In them, personal character is manifested. They are often moments of crisis. They alter the fundamental meaning structures in a person's life. Their effects may be positive or negative. They are like Victor Turner's (1986b, p. 41) "liminal phase of experience." In the liminal, or threshold, moment of experience, the person is in a "no-man's land betwixt and between . . . the past and the . . . future" (p. 41). These are existential acts. Some are ritualized, as in status passages; others are even routinized, as when a man daily batters and beats his wife. Still others are totally emergent and unstructured, and the person enters them with few if any prior understandings of what is going to happen. The meanings of these experiences are always given retrospectively, as they are relived and reexperienced in the stories persons tell about what has happened to them.

Elsewhere (Denzin, 2001, pp. 34–38) I have distinguished four forms of the epiphany: (1) the *major event,* which touches every fabric of a person's life; (2) the cumulative or *representative event,* which signifies eruptions or reactions to experiences which have been going on for a long period of time; (3) the *minor epiphany,* which symbolically represents a major, problematic moment in a relationship or a person's life; and (4) those episodes whose meanings are given in the *reliving* of the experience. I called these, respectively, the major epiphany, the cumulative epiphany, the illuminative or minor epiphany, and the relived epiphany.

The critical autoethnographer enters those strange and familiar situations that connect critical biographical experiences (epiphanies) with culture, history, and social structure. He or she seeks out those narratives and stories people tell one another as they attempt to make sense of the epiphanies, or existential turning-point moments, in their lives. In such moments persons attempt to take history into their own hands, moving into and through, following Turner (1986b), liminal stages of experience.

Epiphanies are experienced as social dramas, as dramatic events with beginnings, middles, and endings. Epiphanies represent ruptures in the structure of daily life. Turner (1986b) reminds us that the theater of social life is often structured around a four-fold processual ritual model involving *breach, crisis, redress, reintegration* or *schism* (p. 41). Each of these phases is organized as a ritual; thus there are rituals of breach, crisis, redress, reintegration and schism. Americans sought rituals of reintegration after 9/11, ways of overcoming the shocks of breach, crisis, and disintegration.

Many rituals and epiphanies are associated with life-crisis ceremonies, "particularly those of puberty, marriage, and death" (Turner, 1986b, p. 41). Turner contends that redressive and life-crisis rituals "contain within themselves a liminal phase, which provides a stage . . . for unique structures of experience" (p. 41). The liminal phase of experience is a kind of no-person's land, on the edge of what is possible, "betwixt and between the structural past and the structural future" (p. 41).

Epiphanies are ritually structured liminal experiences connected to moments of breach, crisis, redress, reintegration and schism, crossing from one space to another.

The storied nature of epiphanic experiences continually raises the following questions: Whose story is being told (and made) here? Who is doing the telling? Who has the authority to make their telling stick (D. E. Smith, 1990a, 1990b)? As soon as a chronological event is told in the form of a story, it enters a text-mediated system of discourse where larger issues of power and control come into play (D. E. Smith, 1990a, 1990b). In this text-mediated system new tellings occur. The interpretations of original experience are now fitted to this larger interpretive structure (D. E. Smith, 1990a, 1990b).

The reflexive performance text contests the pull of traditional "realist" theater and modernist ethnography wherein performers, and ethnographers, reenact and recreate a "recognizable verisimilitude of setting, character and dialogue" (Cohn, 1988, p. 815), where dramatic action reproduces a linear sequence, a "mimetic representation of cause and effect" (Birringer, 1993, p. 196). An evocative epistemology demands a postmodern performance aesthetic that goes beyond "the already-seen and already-heard" (Birringer, 1993, p. 186). This aesthetic criticizes the ideological and technological requirements of late-capitalist social realism and hyperrealism (Birringer, 1993, p. 175). Performances must always return to the lived body (Garoian, 1999; Garoian & Gaudelius 2008). The body's dramaturgical presence is "a site and pretext for . . . debates about representation and gender, about history and postmodern culture" (Birringer, 1993, p. 203). At this level, performance autoethnography answers Trinh's (1991, p. 162) call for works that seek the truth of life's fictions, where experiences are evoked, not explained. The performer seeks a presentation that, like good fiction, is true in experience, but not necessarily true to experience (Lockford, 1998, p. 216).

The body in performance is blood, bone, muscle, movement. "The performing body constitutes its own interpretive presence. It is the raw material of a critical cultural story. The performed body is a cultural text embedded in discourses of power" (Spry, 2011, pp. 18–19). The performing body disrupts the status quo, uncovers "the understory of hegemonic systems" (p. 20).

Whether the events performed actually occurred is tangential to the larger project (Lockford, 1998, p. 216). As dramatic theater, with connections to Brecht (Epic Theater) and Artaud (Theater of Cruelty), these performance texts turn tales of suffering, loss, pain, and victory into evocative performances that have the ability to move audiences to reflective, critical action, not only emotional catharsis (on Brecht's theater, see Benjamin, 1968).

Bill's Story Again

Return to Bill's story. Each form of the epiphany is present. The major forms are seen in Bill's learning how to drink, stopping drinking, seeing God, taking drugs, stealing from his parents, seeing things, going to the mental health clinic. The cumulative, representative, and minor epiphanies are evidenced in his daily trips to the bank and to Al's Pub. Day after day for 3 years, he repeated these experiences as he took his place on the same bar stool and played the same music. Retrospectively, he relives these experiences as he tells them to his A.A. audience. In this telling, he turns back on his life and brings it up to date. In order to make sense out of who Bill is today, we, as listeners, need to know these things about him.

His story as narrative is filled with multiple stories, stories within stories. Each story is organized in terms of an epiphanic moment. There is the story of how he learned to drink and get friends in high school. There are the stories of how he became a hippie, took drugs, built a cabin in the woods, saw God, and fished for salmon. There is the story, which he could tell but only alludes to, about his fear of making change at the bar, so he had to stop at the bank and cash a check for $7.75 every day. These are glossed, indexically understood stories which do not need to be elaborated. Their meanings are contextualized within the framework of the larger story he is telling. They are part of the performance that is called "telling one's story as an alcoholic at an open A.A. meeting." Hence, storytelling is a performative self-act carried out before a group of listeners. The self and personal-experience story is a story-for-a-group. It is a group story.

But more is involved. As Bill speaks, he throws his story out to the audience who hears it. This audience becomes part of the story that is told. A third structure emerges. Not only is Bill talking about his alcoholic self, but he is telling his stories to other alcoholic selves. A group self is formed, a self lodged and located in the performative occasion of the open meeting.

A story that is told is never the same story that is heard. Each teller speaks from a biographical position that is unique and, in a sense, unshareable. Each hearer of a story hears from a similarly unshareable position. But these two versions of the story merge and run together into a collective, group version of the story that was told. Because there are always stories embedded within stories, including the told story and the heard story, there are only multiple versions of shareable and unshareable personal experiences.

When sociologists and other listeners seek to find a common ground of consensual meaning within a story or to establish common meanings that extend across stories, all they end up with are glossed, indexically meaningful, yet depersonalized versions of the life experiences they wish to understand. There is no warrant in such practices.

Stories within stories told to groups remind us that every life story is a multiplicity of stories that could be told. There is no single life story or self-autobiography that grasps or covers all that a life is for a person. There are only multiple stories that can be told. Each storyteller can only tell the stories his or her biography allows to be told. We are, as Heidegger (1962) reminds us, talking beings, and we live and talk our way into being through the poetic, narrative structures of our language. It's not that our language tells our stories for us; rather, we appropriate language for our own discursive purposes. This is what Bill has done.

A doubling of self occurs in Bill's story. He sees himself reflected in the stories he is telling. He becomes a second self within his story, for he is telling a story about himself. This second self is a temporal production, lodged in the past but told in the present. In this temporalizing process, multiple selves speak: the self of the storyteller, the self of the person who built a cabin in Oregon, the self of the recovering alcoholic telling a series of stories about himself, the self telling a story to an open A.A. meeting, and so on. These multiple selves merge, double back, laminate and build on one another, and provide the context and occasion for the production of the larger story that is told.

The boundaries and borders between the multiple stories is never clear-cut, for the meaning of every given story is only given in the difference that separates its beginnings and endings from the story that follows. As one story ends, another begins, but then the earlier story overlaps with the one that is now being told. Stories become arbitrary constructions within the larger narratives that contain the story the teller is attempting to tell.

Bill is producing an oral history, an oral text which is the text of his life at this moment in his personal history. As he does so, he locates himself within the oral storytelling tradition of Western culture. His story follows the narrative outlines of the Western self as it has been reconstituted within the A.A. cultural texts: grace and innocence, fall from grace, and final redemption (Denzin, 1987, pp. 169–170; Misch, 1951). His story is thus continuous with all those other stories that came before his.

The Cultural Locus of Stories

No self or personal-experience story is ever an individual production. It derives from larger group, cultural, ideological, and historical contexts. So it is with Bill's story. His story is located within A.A.'s cultural texts and in the shared history of the A.A. experience. To understand a life, the epiphanies and the personal-experience and self stories that represent and shape that life, one must penetrate and understand these larger structures. They provide the languages, emotions, ideologies, taken-for-granted understandings, and shared experiences from which the stories flow.

The alcoholic's stories emanate from three broad group structures: the family, A.A., and the group before whom the story is told. For A.A. storytellers like Bill, the A.A. group and the A.A. cultural texts define the broad outlines of the self story. But behind every alcoholic stands a family and a structure of family experiences which have become part of his or her story. An unraveling of a story such as Bill's involves an unraveling of the family history that is part of his self.

The A.A. audience members who heard Bill's story had, on different occasions, learned the following facts about his family history: (1) his mother is a recovering alcoholic and suffers from bipolar disorder, as does Bill, who is on medication; (2) his father is an autocratic family patriarch; (3) his sister suffers from bipolar disorder and is employed as a social worker; (4) his brother is getting his PhD; (5) his mother fears for his sanity, fears that he will never complete his higher education program and get a job, feels that he doesn't know how to relate to women and, hence, will probably never get married.

With this knowledge in hand, the audience heard more of Bill's story then he told. They knew that the glossed family history briefly mentioned in his larger story contained references to his mother, brother, father, sister, and to his own history of mental illness. These taken-for-granted understandings constituted a frame of reference for understanding the larger story that was told and heard. A culturally understood self, a self grounded in the culturally expected references to family, drinking, and recovery, was produced in and through Bill's talk. A sociological listener unfamiliar with these features of Bill's personal history would not have heard these things.

Limits of the Story

A story is always an interpretive account, but, of course, all interpretations are biased. However, many times a storyteller neglects important structural factors which have impinged on his or her life. Or if such forces are addressed, they are interpreted from the teller's biased point of view. Many times a person will act as if he or she made his or her own history when, in fact, he or she was forced to make the history he or she lived (Denzin, 1986). The following speaker does this:

> You know I made the last four months by myself. I haven't used or drank. I'm really proud of myself. I did it.

A friend, listening to this account commented:

> You know you were under a court order all last year. You didn't do this on your own. You were forced to, whether you want to accept this fact or not. You also went to A.A. and N.A. Listen Buster. You did what you did because you had help and because you were afraid and thought you had no other choice. Don't give me this, "I did it on my own" crap! (Denzin, 1986, p. 334)

The speaker replies, "I know. I just don't like to admit it."

This listener invokes two structural forces, the state and A.A., which accounted in part this speaker's experiences. To have secured only the speaker's account, without a knowledge of his biography and personal history, would have produced a biased interpretation of his situation.

Process, Structure, and Stories

A story is always an interpretive account, but, of course, all interpretations are biased. The intent of the biographical project is to uncover the social, economic, cultural, structural, and historical forces that shape, distort, and otherwise alter problematic lived experiences (Bertaux, 1981, p. 4). This focus on structure must never lose sight of the individuals who live these structurally shaped lives. On the other hand, subjectivity must not be romanticized.

Now consider another story. Gary, a self-defined addict and alcoholic, is speaking in a closed A.A. meeting, which means that only persons who call themselves alcoholics are present.

Gary's Story

I've lied to you people for six months. I got drunk last night and used cocaine. I've been getting high every day that I've been coming here. I use cocaine in the morning, before I go to meetings and at night. I guess I'm an addict. When I told my story at the area breakfast [the same open meeting Bill told his story to], I neglected to say that I had been using cocaine every day. I guess I was lying. . . . I think I need to get honest with myself. But I don't know how. I've lied to myself for so long I don't know what's true and what's false.

True and False Stories?

Gary's story brings us, once again, to the problems of truth and the accurate representations of a life and its experiences. By his own admission, he has been lying to the A.A. group for months. He has also been lying to himself. He would be the first person to say that he cannot tell the difference between what is a lie and what is the truth.

Several problems are at work in this account. The stories other alcoholics heard Gary tell were heard-as-true stories, although some listeners may have expected that he was lying. To tell a story that is heard as true, means that the speaker must know the group's criteria for what is true and what is false and know how to present a self that will be in conformity with the group's conceptions and standards of truthfulness. A story heard as true becomes part of the teller's public biography. Gary knew how to tell such a story. He was seen as having built up 6 months of "clean and sober" time. He was told by others that he was doing well, that he was making great strides in his program. As he heard these comments, he knew—or a part of him knew—that he was using cocaine and was not the clean and sober person he was presenting himself as being.

Knowing how a true story is told, Gary is now confronted with the problem of telling a story that truthfully states that he has been lying. He needs to tell a story that discounts the false stories he has been telling. In order to convince his listeners that he is now telling the truth, he has to convince them that he had earlier been telling lies. A false story can only be discredited by another story, which requires that it be heard as a true story. He does this by stating that he was using cocaine over the period of time he said that he was clean and sober.

Assuming that Gary is now telling the truth, and assuming that the group assumes that he is now telling the truth, how do self story researchers know when and if the stories they hear are true or false? Faulkner reminds the readers of his trilogy on the Snopes family that not even Flem Snopes told himself what he was up to. How do we know what we are up to when we are hearing stories told by persons who may not know what they are up to? This problem extends beyond the validity or the factual accuracy of a story. It involves processes that cut to the core of what it means to be a person who is able to tell stories about himself or herself.

Every storyteller has two options when telling a story: to tell a story that accords with the fictional facts about his or her life or to tell a story that departs from those facticities. Sociologists as listeners are seldom in a position to tell the difference between these two narrative forms. This is acutely the case when the teller has learned the cultural ways of the social group from whose structures his or her story comes.

Now Becker (1986) reminds us that "knowledge is relative . . . and *is* what I can get other people to accept . . . but that truth need not be the *whole* truth . . . [and] the question is whether . . . X *and only* X is true, or . . . that, while X is true, Y is too" (pp. 3, 280, 294, italics in original). Gary's stories were both true and false: He hadn't been drinking, except for the night before he told this story (true), but he had been using, when he said he had been clean and sober (false).

Many groups aren't as loose as Becker. They want truthful statements that apply to every instance of a phenomenon, not to just some of them. They want X and only X to be true, and not X and sometimes Y and then sometimes Z. In A.A., you are either clean and sober or you are not. So while knowledge and truth are relative across groups and settings, within settings they often are not. Researchers must establish the criteria of truth that operate in the groups that are studied. It will be these criteria that structure the stories that are told by the group members.

Here is the dilemma. There are only interpretations, and all that people tell are self stories. The sociologist's task cannot be one of determining the difference between true and false stories. All stories, as argued earlier, are fictions. The sociologist's task, then, involves studying how persons and their groups culturally produce warrantable self and personal-experience stories which accord with that group's standards of truth. We study how persons learn how to tell stories which match a group's understandings of what a story should look and sound like. It seems that little more can or needs to be said on this matter of truthfulness and knowing.

I have thus far attempted to establish the following points: (1) stories and the performances they are attached to always come in multiple versions, and they never have clear endings or beginnings; (2) stories and performances are grounded in a group's culture where criteria of truthfulness are established; (3) the stories told are never the same as the stories heard; (4) stories are shaped by larger ideological forces which put pressure on persons to establish their individuality (and self-control) in the stories they construct.

Mystory as Montage

The performed text is lived experience, and lived experiences in two senses (Pelias, 1999). The performance doubles back on the experiences previously represented in the writer's text. It then re-presents those experiences as an embodied performance. It thus privileges immediate experience, the evocative moment when another's experiences come alive for performers and audiences alike. One way the performed text is given narrative meaning in interpretive autoethnography is through the mystory.

The mystory is simultaneously a personal mythology, a public story, a personal narrative, and a performance that critiques. It is an interactive, dramatic performance. It is participatory theater, a performance, not a text-centered interpretive event; that is, the emphasis is on performance and improvisation, and not on the reading of a text.

The mystory is a montage text, cinematic and multimedia in shape, filled with sounds, music, poetry, and images taken from the writer's personal history. This personal narrative is grafted into discourses from popular culture. It locates itself against the specialized knowledges that circulate in the larger society. The audience co-performs the text, and the writer, as narrator, functions as a guide, a commentator, a co-performer.

Focusing on epiphanies and liminal moments of experience, the writer imposes a narrative framework on the text. This framework shapes how experience will be represented. It uses the devices of plot, setting, characters, characterization, temporality, dialogue, protagonists, antagonists—showing, not telling. The narration may move through Turner's four-stage dramatic cycle, emphasizing breach, crisis, redress, reintegration or schism.

Jameson (1990) reminds us that works of popular culture are always already ideological and utopian. Shaped by a dialectic of anxiety and hope, such works revive and manipulate fears and anxieties about the social order. Beginning with a fear, problem, or crisis, these works move characters and audiences through the familiar three-stage dramatic model of conflict, crisis, and resolution. In this way they offer kernels of utopian hope. They show how these anxieties and fears can be satisfactorily addressed by the existing social order. Hence, the audience is lulled into believing that the problems of the social have in fact been successfully resolved.

The mystory occupies a similar ideological space, except it functions as critique. The mystory is also ideological and utopian; it begins from a progressive political position stressing the politics of hope. The mystory uses the methods of performance and personal narrative to present its critique and utopian vision. It presumes that the social order has to change if problems are to be successfully resolved in the long run. If the status quo is maintained, if only actors, and not the social order, change, then the systemic processes producing the problem remain in place. We are left then with just our stories and the performances of them.

Staging Lives[2]

In the summer of 1953 I was 12 and my brother Mark was 8.[7] This was the summer my parents divorced for the first time. This was also the summer my father joined Alcoholics Anonymous. Mark and I were spending the summer on the farm with Grandpa and Grandma.

This was the summer

of the Joseph McCarthy Hearings

on television, black and white screens.

Eisenhower was president,

Nixon was his vice-president.

This was the summer Grandpa bought the first family TV.

In the afternoons

we watched the McCarthy Hearings,

and each evening

we had a special show to watch:

Ed Sullivan on Sundays,

Milton Berle and Cardinal Sheen on Mondays,

Norman Vincent Peale and Pat Boone on Tuesday.

This was the summer my parents

divorced for the first time.

This was the summer my father's life started to fall apart.

I look today at the face of Joseph McCarthy

in George Clooney's movie, Good Night and Good Luck,

a scared lonely man,

Clooney's movie tells me McCarthy died from alcoholism.

I thought of that summer of 1953 and Clooney's movie as I was going through Dad's scrapbook. The pictures are all from the late 40s and early 50s. Mark and I were little and living with Grandpa and Grandma. Mother and Dad lived in Coralville, just outside Iowa City. Dad was a county agent for the Farm Bureau, and Mother kept house and was ill a lot.

I think this is when Dad's drinking

started to get out of hand.

He'd work late, come home drunk.

Some nights friends from work drove him home.

Mother and Dad had put knotty pine siding

on the walls of the family rec room,

which was in the basement of our new house.

Dad built a bar,

And mother got cocktail glasses, a blender,

shot glasses, glass coasters—

really fancy stuff.

On the weekends men from the insurance agency

brought their wives over,

and the house was filled with smoke, laughter,

and Benny Goodman and Harry James

on a little Philco phonograph.

Fats Domino was on the jukeboxes

Singing "Ain't That a Shame" and "Blueberry Hill."

Mother was drinking pretty heavily.

She liked manhattans and maraschino cherries.

Dad drank Pabst Blue Ribbon (a "Blue"),

and straight shots of Jim Beam whiskey.

Around this time the Communist scare had gotten all the way to Iowa City. World War III was on the horizon. The John Birch Society was gaining strength. *This Is Your FBI, The Lone Ranger, The Shadow*, and *Inner Sanctum* were popular radio and TV shows. We were all learning how to be imaginary consumers in this new culture: Gillette Blue Blades, Bulova Time, Lava Soap, Life Savers (Dylan, 2004).

Citizen Civil Defense Groups were forming.

People were worried about Communists,

and air attacks at night,

atomic bombs going off in big cities.

People started building bomb shelters.

Dad built a shelter in the back yard.

Every town had a Civilian Civil Defense team.

Dad was a team leader,

gone from midnight

until 6:00 in the morning two times a week.

He stood guard with a three other men,

scanning the skies with binoculars and telescopes

looking for low-flying Russian planes.

He would come home drunk.

Bob Dylan wrote a song about this post-WWII paranoia: He called it "Talkin' John Birch Paranoid Blues." In it, Eisenhower is a Russian spy.

We became an A.A. family in 1953. The drinking had gone too far. About one year later, Mom and Dad had some A.A. friends out for a cookout on the farm.

There was a new couple, Shirley and George. Shirley had black hair like mom, and she was small and petite. She was wearing an orange dress that flowed all around her knees. Dad set up the archery set behind the lilacs in the side yard. The men gathered with bows and you could hear the twang of the arrows all the way back in the house. But nobody was very good.

Mom had Pete Fountain and his clarinet playing on the portable record player. Everybody came back in the house, and before you knew it the dining room was filled with dancing couples. Men and women in 1950s dress-up clothes, wide-collar shirts, pleated slacks, and greased-back hair. Women with Mamie Eisenhower bangs, hose, garter belts, and high heels.

All of sudden Dad was dancing with Shirley, and Mom was in the kitchen fixing snacks. I thought Dad and Shirley were dancing a little close to just be friends.

About a month later our little world changed forever. I came home from high school and found a note from Dad. It was short and read, "I have to leave you. You and Mark are on your own now." I was 18 and Mark was 14.

Civilian Civil Defense teams,

Bomb shelters,

Talking John Birch Society paranoia,

The CIA, the Cold War, Communists, the Axis of Evil,

another war, global terror, an out of control right wing government.

My father's life segues into this question, "What went wrong with our generation's and our parents' generation's version of the American Dream?" And like in George Clooney's movie, good luck was no longer enough, even if Mamie Eisenhower did wear bangs, just like my grandmother, and even if my father kept the United States safe from the Communists.

Back to the Beginning

Today I want to write my way out of this history, and this is why I write my version of performance autoethnography. I want to push back, intervene, be vulnerable, tell another story. I want to contest what happened (Pelias, 2011, p. 12).

I want to return to the memories of my childhood, fish fries along the Iowa River, horseback rides along Clear Creek in early spring, that Sunday morning when my family visited the Mesquaki Reservation. We were happy that day. Alcoholism had not yet hit our little house, but A.A. was not far off. As a family we were slipping. A day on the reservation brought escape from what was coming. Could things have happened differently if my father had stopped drinking on that day? I know my brother and I fought, and we were not grateful. Could my father and mother have recovered a love that day that would have withstood infidelities and drunkenness? Did Indians have anything at all to do with this? Maybe an alternative ending is fruitless; why even try?

I think I'm like the narrator in Guy Maddin's 2007 film *My Winnipeg*.[3] In the film Maddin returns to his family home and rents the house for a month so he can redo some things that happened in that house when he was 12 years old.[4] He hires actors to play his mother, father, brother, and sister. He rents a pet dog. When the month is up, there are still issues that have not been resolved.

I could be like Gay Maddin. I'd rent the Iowa farmhouse for a week, the house where Dad and Shirley danced too close, and I'd have mom tell Shirley to take her hands off of her husband. Or maybe I'd go back to the little house on Coralville and have Dad and Mom pretend that they didn't have to be drinking in order to act as if they loved each other.

Performing the Text: Writing to Change History[5]

The goal is to produce an interruption, a performance text that challenges conventional taken-for-granted assumptions about the racialized past. Let's return to Indians, Squanto, Tonto, and to my opening scenes with Mr. Thomas and the Fox Reservation. For example, in my current research (Denzin, 2008, 2011, 2013a) I criticize the representations of Native Americans by such 19th century artists as George Catlin and Charles Bird King. I also critically read William Cody's (aka Buffalo Bill) Wild West Shows, which staged performances by Native Americans in Europe and America from 1882 to 1910.

Recurring figures in my narrative include the voices of marginalized Native Americans, including Ms. Birdie Berdashe,[6] a two-spirit person, an aboriginal dandy, a man who assumes a female gender identity painted by George Catlin; Miss Chief, the drag-queen alter ego of Cree artist Kent Monkman; Lonesome Rider, a gay cowboy; Virile Dandy, a Mandan warrior, close friend of Birdie Berdashe; and the LGBT Chorus. These figures literally and figuratively "queer" my text (Adams & Jones, 2008, p. 383). These transgressive figures challenge the stereotype of the masculine heterosexual Indian warrior. They refuse to be submissive. Miss Chief and Ms. Birdie bring agency and power to queer Indians who were mocked and ridiculed by Catlin, King, and Cody. Imagine these queer Indians dancing on the Fox Reservation.

Here is a sample text. It appears at the end of a four-act play titled "The Traveling Indian Gallery, Part Two." In the play, 35 Fox, Iowa, and Ojibwe tribe members, along with the LGBT Chorus, Birdie, Miss Chief, and Lonesome Rider, contest their place in Catlin's Traveling European Indian Gallery (1843–1846). The play culminates in a play-within-the-play on stage outside the Boudoir Berdashe. Fox Indians, perhaps related to the Fox Indians my brother and I saw dance in the Reservation Pow Wow in 1950, perform in Catlin's play. The excerpt begins with Birdie.

Birdie: Before we walk off this stupid stage I want to do a "Dance for the Berdashe." George called it an "unaccountable and ludicrous custom amongst the Sacs and Foxes which admits not of an entire explanation" (Catlin, 1848, p. 286).

Virile Dandy: The dance honors the power of the Berdashe. In his painting, George demeans the Berdashe, contrasting his/her passive femininity with the raw, virile masculinity of the bare-chested male dancers who are wearing loincloths and holding weapons.

Narrator: At this point I try to remember back to the Pow Wow. I wonder if we only saw bare-chested warriors waving weapons. What if a young two-spirited Fox was also one of the dancers? Would we have been able to identify him/her and understand his/her place in the tribe's hierarchy of male/female identities?

(Off-stage: The Hot Club of Cow Town, a Cowboy swing band from Austin, Texas, breaks into a slow-dance waltz, "Darling You and I Are Through."[7] At the opposite end of the hall, the All-Star Sac and Fox Drummer and Dance Band [from IndigeNOW[8]] begins playing a soft blues ballad led by Clyde Roulette [Ojibway], aka Slidin Clyde Roulette, blues guitarist.[9])

(Stage directions: The stage is transformed into a dance floor, the lights dim. The members of the LGBT and Indian Show Choruses pair off as couples, men waltz with men, women with women, men with women, children with children. Off come Berdashe masks. Bodies swirl around the dance floor. Virile Dandy dares to take the Queen by her hand and put his arm around her waist, leading her in a two-step waltz across the stage.)

In this excerpt the Native American players mock and queer the concept of the straight Indian performing as an Indian for a White Anglo-European audience. They turn the performance event upside down; in so doing they expose and criticize a racist heterosexualist politics buried deep inside the 19th century colonizing imaginary. This performance bleeds into the earlier Native American narratives. Surely there were queer or two-spirited Indians on the reservation, but they were not visible to a young White boy on that Sunday in 1950.

Like Guy Maddin I'd try to go back and redo that Pow Wow. I'd bring in Berdie, Virile Dandy, and the LGBT Chorus. I'd have Indian vendors sell cheap copies of George Catlin's paintings of Fox Indians. I'd write myself into the storyline and tell my parents that I think we should not go to these kinds of performances.

Working to Transgress

The goal is to create a safe space where writers, teachers, and students are willing to take risks, to move back and forth between the personal and the political, the biographical and the historical. In these spaces they perform painful personal experiences. Under this framework we teach one another. We push against racial, sexual, and class boundaries in order to achieve the gift of freedom; the gift of love, self-caring; the gift of empowerment, teaching and learning to transgress. We talk about painful experiences, those moments where race, class, gender, sexuality intersect. We take these risks because we have created safe space for such performances—from classrooms, to conference sessions, to the pages of journals, and in our books—and the payoff is so great. We are free in these spaces to explore painful experiences, to move forward into new spaces, into new identities, new relationships, new, radical forms of scholarship, new epiphanies.

This is performance-centered pedagogy that uses performance as a method of investigation, as a way of doing autoethnography, and as a method of understanding. Mystory, performance, ethnodrama, and reality theater are ways of making visible the oppressive structures of the culture—racism, homophobia, sexism (Saldana, 2005, 2011). The performance of these autoethnographic dramas becomes a tool for documenting oppression, a method for understanding the meanings of the oppression, and a way of enacting a politics of possibility.

The pedagogical model I offer is collaborative. It is located in a moral community created out of the interactions and experiences that occur inside and outside the walls of the seminar room. In this safe space scholars come together on the terrain of social justice. While this is done in the sacred safe spaces of collaborative discourse, the fear of criticism and misunderstanding is always present. When they occur, we seek pedagogies of forgiveness.

The lives and stories that we hear and study are given to us under a promise, that promise being that we protect those who have shared with us. And in return, this sharing will allow us to write life documents that speak to the human dignity, the suffering, the hopes, the dreams, the lives gained, and the lives lost by the people we study. These documents will become testimonies to the ability of the human being to endure, to prevail, and to triumph over the structural forces that threaten at any moment to annihilate all of us. If we foster the illusion that we understand when we do not or that we have found meaningful, coherent lives where none exist, then we engage in a cultural practice that is just as repressive as the most repressive of political regimes.

Notes

1. This section draws on materials in Denzin (2001, pp. 38–39; 2003, pp. 42–44).
2. This section draws on Denzin (2010, pp. 62–67).
3. Maddin is a well-known Canadian filmmaker. *My Winnipeg* was awarded the prize for Best Canadian Feature Film in 2007. Materials in this section draw from Denzin (2013b).
4. His pet dog died. His sister had a big fight with his mother. His father may have died.
5. This section draws from materials in Chapters 3 and 4 in Denzin (2013a).
6. My name. An American or First Nation Indian who assumes the dress, social status, and role of the opposite sex (see Califia, 1997).
7. From the first album (*Swingin' Stampede*) by the Hot Club of Cowtown, the Texas Jazz/Western Swing Trio from Austin, Texas.
8. Compliments of IndigeNOW with Gordon Bronitsky and Associates.
9. Clyde sounds a little like Stevie Ray Vaughn. He recently played with the Neville Brothers in Sioux City, Iowa.

5

Reading and Writing Interpretation[1]

Written and performed autoethnography has the power to actually insist on mutual respect in embodied and textual encounters between ourselves and those "others" our cultures and beliefs have alienated and misrecognized. (Gingrich-Philbrook, 2013, p. 612)

For qualitative researchers, the turn to performance autoethnographic texts poses the problem of performative criteria, namely how these texts and their performances are to be critically analyzed in terms of epistemological, aesthetic, and political criteria. Building on recent discussions of interpretive criteria (Jones, Adams, & Ellis, 2013b; Madison, 2012) I foreground subversive, resistance narratives—dramatic, epiphanic performances that challenge the status quo.[2] My topics are reading, writing, and judging performances and producing autoethnographic performances that move history.

My argument unfolds in four parts. I begin with a discussion of criticisms of the genre and responses to the criticisms. I then turn to the problem of setting criteria for experimental writing (Bochner, 2000; Bochner & Riggs, in press; Clough, 2000, 2007; Faulkner, 2009; Gingrich-Philbrook, 2013; Richardson, 2000b). This leads to a discussion of feminist and communitarian criteria as they apply to resistance performance texts. I next discuss alternative modes of assessing narrative and performance texts, building on the recent arguments of Richardson (2000a, 2000b, 2001), Bochner (2000), Ellis (2000), Bochner and Ellis (2002) and Clough (2000). I conclude with commentary on the politics of interpretation in the performance community.

Criticisms and Responses

Autoethnography has been criticized for being nonanalytic, self-indulgent, irreverent, sentimental, and romantic. The focus on the narrative, not the performative I, has also been criticized (Jackson & Mazzei, 2008, p. 299).

Autoethnography has been criticized for being too artful. It has been criticized for not being scientific, for having no theory, no concepts, no hypotheses. It has been criticized for not being sufficiently artful (Ellis, Adams, & Bochner, 2011). It has been dismissed for not being sufficiently rigorous, theoretical, or analytical. Critics contend that a single case only tells one story; narrative inquiry is not scientific inquiry.

Some charge that autoethnographers do too little field work, have small samples, use biased data, are navel-gazers, and are too self-absorbed, offering only verisimilitude, and not analytic insights. Others say it is bad writing. Some contend it reflects the work of a writer who sits in front of a computer, never leaving a book-lined office to confront the real world (see Ellis et al., 2011, for a review of these criticisms). And of course poststructuralists contend that such key terms as *experience, voice, presence*, and *meaning* are undertheorized.

Methodological critics claim autoethnographies lack reliability, generalizability, and validity. Of course these terms come from a positivist framework and have specific meaning within that discourse. Naturally reliability, generalizability, and validity have different meanings (if any) for the autoethnographer (Ellis et al., 2011). This is not traditional ethnography, nor is it performance art.

For the autoethnographer reliability refers to the narrator's credibility as a writer-performer-observer; that is, has an event been correctly remembered and described? Is the writer a credible observer of those events? What does credible even mean? Is the report pure fiction or a truthful account? Autoethnographers assert that narrative truth is based on how a story is used, understood, and responded to. Memory is fallible. People tell different stories of the same event or experience (Ellis et al., 2011).

Validity means that a work has verisimilitude. It evokes a feeling that the experience described is true, coherent, believable, and connects the reader to the writer's world. Stake (1994) calls this naturalistic generalization, the reader "comes to know some things told, as if he or she had experienced them" (p. 240). Generalizability is determined by how a reader responds to a representation. Does it speak to him or her as a universal singular (Ellis et al., 2011)?

Apples and oranges again. Autoethnography cannot be judged by traditional positivist criteria. The goal is not to produce a standard social science article. The goal is to write performance texts in a way that moves others to ethical action.

Setting Criteria for Performance Autoethnography

To repeat, in the social sciences today there is no longer a God's eye view which guarantees absolute methodological certainty. All inquiry reflects the standpoint of the inquirer. All observation is theory-laden. There is no possibility of theory- or value-free knowledge. The days of naive realism and naive positivism are over. In their place stand critical and historical realism and various versions of relativism. The criteria for evaluating research are now relative.

Clough (2000) rightly warns that setting criteria for judging what is good and what is bad experimental writing or performance ethnography may only conventionalize the new writing "and make more apparent the ways in which experimental writing has already become conventional" (p. 278). More deeply, in normalizing this writing, and the performances connected to it, we may forget that this kind of writing was once "thought to be 'bad' writing, improper sociology. . . . It might be forgotten that experimental writing was strongly linked to political contentions over questions of knowledge" (p. 278). And the new writing, in one moment, was taken to be a form of cultural criticism, a way of also criticizing traditional ethnography.

Bochner (2000) elaborates, observing that today "no single, unchallenged paradigm has been established for deciding what does and what does not comprise valid, useful, and significant knowledge" (p. 268). Furthermore, it is impossible to fix a single standard for deciding what is good or bad, or right; there are only multiple standards, temporary criteria, momentary resting places. Too often criteria function as policing devices. The desire to authorize one set of standards can take our attention away from "the ethical issues at the heart of our work" (p. 269).

On this point Clough (2000) and Christians (2000) agree with Bochner: All inquiry involves moral, political and ethical matters. Clough goes one level deeper. She reminds us that from the beginning, the criticisms of standard ethnographic writing in sociology were linked to identity politics and feminist theory, and in anthropology to postcolonial criticisms. These criticisms involved a complex set of questions, namely who had the right to speak for whom and how (Clough, 2000, p. 283).

The need to represent postcolonial hybrid identities became the focus of experimental writing in ethnography, just as there has been "an effort to elaborate race, classed, sexed, and national identities in the autoethnographic writings of postcolonial theorists" (Clough, 2000, p. 285; see also Madison, 2012, pp. 236–237). These debates about writing, agency, self, subjectivity, nation, culture, race, and gender unfolded on a global landscape, involving the transnationalization of capital and the globalization of technology (Clough, 2000, p. 279). Thus from the beginning, experimental autoethnographic writing has been closely connected to gender, race, family, nation, politics, capital, technology, critical social theory, and cultural criticism; that is, to debates over questions of knowledge, and its representation and presentation.

The drive to performance autoethnography within Western ethnography, the drive to the personal and the autobiographical, Clough suggests, reflects a growing sensitivity to issues surrounding agency and the new media technologies. But the subjectivity and forms of selfhood performed and examined in the new autoethnography are linked to "the trauma culture of the teletechnological" (Clough, 2000, p. 287; see also Halley, 2012, pp. 5–6). Clough (2000) observes that much of the new autoethnography involves persons writing about the "experiences of drug abuse, sexual abuse, child abuse, rape, incest, anorexia, chronic illness, and death" and that "autoethnography is symptomatic of the trauma culture that has been most outrageously presented in television talk shows" (p. 287; see also Clough, 2007, pp. 2–3, 5).

This trauma culture exposes and celebrates the erasure of traditional barriers separating the public and the private in American life. In a pornography of the visible, the violent side of intimate family life is exposed, and the contradictions in capitalism as a way of life are revealed. Much of the new autoethnography focuses on trauma, on injuries, on troubled, repressed memories, inabilities to speak the past, the search for a new voice, shattered, damaged egos seeking new histories, new forms of agency. But in speaking from the spaces of trauma, autoethnographers do not "critically or self-consciously engage enough the technical substrata of their own writing form" (Clough, 2000, p. 287).

Clough (2000) does not mean to trivialize the trauma written about; rather, she wants to read it as symptomatic of something else that requires attention, namely how the new television, computer, and media technologies, in conjunction with global capital on a transnational scale, are creating new forms of subjectivity. "I think it is these figures of subjectivity appearing in autoethnography which cultural criticism must now attend" (p. 287).

Thus Clough (2000) comes back to a single criterion for evaluating experimental writing: cultural criticism and theoretical reflection. Staying close to these two terms allows "experimental writing to be a vehicle for thinking new sociological subjects, new parameters of the social" (p. 290). She is fearful that the search for new criteria will silence cultural criticism. I agree.

Mindful of the above distinctions, discussions of criteria move in three directions at the same time: moral, political, and ethical; literary and aesthetic; trauma and the politics of experience.

Feminist, Communitarian Criteria

Building on Clough and Madison, the understandings and criteria for evaluating critical performance events combine aesthetics, ethics, and epistemologies.[3] Several criteria can be outlined. Like hooks's (1990, p. 111) black aesthetic and Giroux's (2001, p. 25) public pedagogy, these performance criteria erase the usual differences between ethics, politics, and power. This erasure creates the possibilities for a practical, performative pedagogy, a call for performances which intervene and interrupt public life. Such interruptions are meant to unsettle and challenge taken-for-granted assumptions concerning problematic issues in public life. They create a space for dialogue and questions, giving a voice to positions previously silenced or ignored.

Ideologically, this performance aesthetic refuses assimilation to White middle-class norms and the traumas of that culture. It resists those understandings that valorize performances and narratives centered on the life crises of the humanistic subject. In contrast, this aesthetic values performance narratives that reflexively go against the grain and attack the dominant cultural ideologies connected to nation, race, class, family, and gender. These performances expose cracks in the ideological seams in these dominant cultural mythologies.

Three interconnected criteria shape these representations of the world. *Interpretive sufficiency* is the watchphrase (Christians, 2000, p. 145).[4] Accounts should possess that amount of depth, detail, emotionality, nuance, and coherence that will permit the formation of a critical consciousness, or what Paulo Freire (2000) terms *conscientization*. Through conscientization the oppressed gain their own voice and collaborate in transforming their culture (Christians, 2000, p. 148).

Second, these accounts should exhibit a *representational adequacy* and be free of racial, class, or gender stereotyping (Christians, 2000, p. 145). Finally texts are *authentically adequate* when three conditions are met: (1) they represent multiple voices, (2) they enhance moral discernment, and (3) they promote social transformation (Christians, 2000, p. 145). Multivoiced ethnographic texts should empower persons, leading them to discover moral truths about themselves while generating social criticism. These criticisms, in turn, should lead to efforts at social transformation (Christians, 2000, p. 147).

This is a dialogical epistemology and aesthetic. It involves a give and take, an ongoing moral dialogue between persons. It enacts an ethic of care and an ethic of personal and communal responsibility (Collins, 1991, p. 214). Politically, this aesthetic imagines how a truly democratic society might look, including one free of racial prejudice and oppression. This aesthetic values beauty and artistry, movement, rhythm, color, and texture in everyday life. It celebrates difference and the sounds of many different voices. It expresses an ethic of empowerment.

This ethic presumes a moral community that is ontologically prior to the person. This community has shared moral values, including the concepts of shared governance, neighborliness, love, kindness, and the moral good

(Christians, 2000, pp. 144–149). This ethic embodies a sacred, existential epistemology that locates persons in a noncompetitive, nonhierarchical relationship to the larger moral universe. This ethic declares that all persons deserve dignity and a sacred status in the world. It stresses the value of human life, truth telling, and nonviolence (Christians, 2000, p. 147).

Under the principle of authentic adequacy, this aesthetic enables social criticism and engenders resistance. It helps persons imagine how things could be different. It imagines new forms of human transformation and emancipation. It enacts these transformations through dialogue. If necessary, it sanctions nonviolent forms of civil disobedience (Christians, 2000, p. 148). In asking that interpretive work provide the foundations for social criticism and social action, this ethic represents a call to action.

This aesthetic understands that moral criteria are always fitted to the contingencies of concrete circumstances, assessed in terms of those local understandings that flow from feminist, communitarian understandings. This ethic calls for dialogical research rooted in the concepts of care and shared governance. How this ethic works in any specific situation cannot be given in advance.

Literary and Aesthetic Criteria

I turn now to the work of Ellis, Bochner, and Richardson. Collectively these scholars offer a subtly nuanced set of criteria that emphasize the literary, substantive, and aesthetic dimensions of the new writing. In the main, these scholars and their students have focused on what Clough calls the experiences embedded in the culture of trauma. Their works (especially those of Ellis and Bochner) destigmatize the experiences of damaged egos.

Ellis (2000, p. 273; 2009, pp. 14–17), Ellis et al. (2011), and Jones et al. (2013b) offer a fully developed literary aesthetic. Ellis and her coauthors want writing that conforms to the criteria of interpretive sufficiency and authentic adequacy. They want works that are engaging and nuanced, texts that allow readers to feel. They want a story that immerses readers in another world, a story that stays with the reader after she or he has read it. Ellis privileges evocation over cognitive contemplation. If writers cannot write evocatively, she recommends they write in another genre. She asks that a story tell her something new: "about social life, social process, the experience of others, the author's experience, my own life. Is there anything 'new' here?" (Ellis, 2000, p. 275).

To the criteria of interpretive sufficiency and authentic adequacy, Ellis adds a third, what might be called literary value, or what Richardson (2000a, p. 254; 2000b, p. 937) calls aesthetic merit. Ellis wants stories to have a good plot; to have dramatic tension; to be coherent, logically consistent; to exhibit balance, flow, and an authenticity of experience; to be lifelike. She asks that authors show and not tell, that they develop characters and scenes fully, but that there not be too many characters or scenes.

Ellis (2000, p. 276) wants careful editing, an economy of words, but vivid pictures, sounds, smells, feelings, conversations that feel like real life, surprise endings that challenge her to see things in a new way. She asks if analysis has been connected closely to the story and to the relevant literature. She asks if the story is worth fighting for, even if it is unconventional.

Ellis (2000, p. 275) wants to know what the author's goals are, what he or she is trying to achieve, and asks if the goals are achievable and if they are worthwhile. She asks if another writing form would better serve the author's purposes. She wonders if the writer learned anything new about himself or herself, about other characters in the story, about social processes and relationships.

A *relational ethics* is advocated, an ethics that asks researchers to act from their hearts and minds; to be caring, open inquirers; to bring respect and dignity to the researcher relationship. Relational ethics recognizes that relationships change over time and that ethical obligations change accordingly (Ellis, 2009, p. 308; Ellis et al., 2011). Autoethnographers are obligated to share their work with those others who are implicated in their texts, including giving them space to talk back (Ellis, 2000, p. 275).

Bochner's Narratives of Self

Ellis's literary realism compliments Bochner's vision of poetic social science and alternative ethnography. Bochner also emphasizes issues surrounding interpretive sufficiency. He asks if these new narratives of self use language in a way that allows the reader (and writer) to extract meaning from experience, "rather than depict experience exactly as it was lived" (Bochner, 2000, p. 270). Bochner isolates seven criteria.

First, he looks for abundant, concrete detail, for the "flesh and blood emotions of people coping with life's contingencies; not only facts but also feelings" (Bochner, 2000, p. 270). Second, he likes structurally complex narratives, stories told in the curve of time, weaving past and present together in the nonlinear spaces of memory work. Third, he judges authors in terms of their emotional credibility, vulnerability, and honesty. He wants texts that comment on those "cultural scripts that resist transformation . . . squeezing comedy out of life's tragedies," texts that take a "measure of life's limitations" (p. 270). Fourth, he wants stories of two selves, stories of who I was to who I am, lives transformed by crisis.

Fifth, Bochner (2000) holds the writer to "a demanding standard of ethical self-consciousness" (p. 271). Like Ellis, he wants the writer to show concern for those who are written about, concern for their place in the story, concern for how telling the story changes the writer's (and reader's) self, concern for the "moral commitments and convictions that underlie the story" (p. 271). Sixth, also like Ellis, he wants a story that "moves me, my heart and belly as well as my head" (p. 271). He does not demean a story if it is confessional or erotic, or pornographic, because every story is a dare, a risk.

Seventh, consistent with the criteria of authentic adequacy, Bochner (2000) wants narratives of the self that can be used as "a source of empowerment and a form of resistance to counter the domination of canonical discourses" (p. 271). He values those works that devictimize stigmatized identities, works that "confirm and humanize tragic experience by bearing witness to what it means to live with shame, abuse, addiction, or bodily dysfunction and to gain agency through testimony" (p. 271).

These criteria do not actively engage the issues surrounding authentic adequacy, including ethical discernment and social transformation. It is perhaps not enough, Clough would argue, to just bear witness to tragic experience, to just make public the traumas of the trauma culture.

Richardson's Five Criteria

Laurel Richardson (2000a) asks for more, offering five criteria that move back and forth across the dimensions of interpretive sufficiency, representational adequacy, and authentic adequacy. Her first criterion is *substantive contribution*: Does the piece contribute to our understanding of social life? Is the work grounded in a social scientific perspective? Second, she asks if the work has *aesthetic merit*: Does it succeed aesthetically, is it artistically shaped, is it satisfying, complex, not boring (p. 254)? Her third criterion is *reflexivity*, which involves several separate issues. She asks if the author is familiar with the epistemology of postmodernism. She wants to know how the information in the text was gathered; were ethical issues involved in this process? She asks if the author's subjectivity is in the text, is the point of view clear, is there adequate self-awareness and self-exposure. Is the author held accountable to standards of knowing and telling (p. 254).

The fourth criterion assesses *impact*. Richardson (2000b) asks how the work affects her emotionally, intellectually, and as a scholar. Does it generate new questions? Does it move her to try new research practices? Does it move her to action? Fifth, she wants to know how the work *expresses a reality*. "Does this text embody a fleshed out, embodied sense of lived-experience? Does it seem 'true'—a credible account of a cultural, social, individual, or communal sense of the 'real'" (p. 937)?

Together, Ellis, Bochner, and Richardson offer a set of interpretive criteria that emphasize the literary and aesthetic qualities of a work as well as its substantive contributions to an area of knowledge. Ethically, they focus on the dialogical relationship between the writer and the subject, asking that this be an honest and open relationship. Each of these scholars wants to be moved emotionally and intellectually by a work. Each values reflexivity and texts that empower.

A new aesthetic criterion emerges in this reading of Ellis, Bochner, and Richardson. It might be termed the dialogical requirement. In asking that they be moved by a text, these writers want works that invite them into another person's world of experience. In privileging the reading experience, they bring new meaning to the writerly text. If writing is a form of inquiry, then they want works that provoke self-reflection.

Faulkner's Criteria

Faulkner (2009, p. 89), drawing on Richardson (2000a), Ellis (2000), Bochner (2000), Clough (2000), and others, sets out three criteria for evaluating research poetry:[5]

scientific criteria: depth, authenticity, trustworthiness, understanding, reflexivity, usefulness, articulation of method, ethics

poetic criteria: artistic concentration, embodied experience, discovery, conditional, narrative truth, transformation

artistic criteria: compression of data, understanding of craft, social justice, moral truth, emotional verisimilitude, sublime, empathy

Faulkner's first two categories are applied to any form of critical qualitative inquiry. Her third category can be extended. Is the performance text effective aesthetically? Does it exhibit accessible literary qualities? Is it dramatically evocative? Is it lyrical? Does it invoke shared feelings, images, scenes, and memories? Does it express emotion effectively, economically? Does it establish *objective correlatives* for the emotions the writer is attempting to evoke (see Eliot, 1922)? Does it meet the criteria attributed to Emily Dickenson: " If I read a work and it makes my whole body so cold no fire can ever warm me, I know it is poetry."

Performative Criteria

Building on the above normative understandings, I value those autoethnographic performance texts that do the following:

1. Unsettle, criticize, and challenge taken-for-granted, repressed meanings

2. Invite moral and ethical dialogue while reflexively clarifying their own moral position

3. Engender resistance and offer utopian thoughts about how things can be made different

4. Demonstrate that they care, that they are kind

5. Show, instead of tell, while using the rule that less is more

6. Exhibit interpretive sufficiency, representational adequacy, and authentic adequacy

7. Are political, functional, collective, and committed

In asking if a performance event does these things, I understand that every performance is different. Further, audiences may or may not agree on what is caring, or kind, or reflexive, and some persons may not want their taken-for-granted understandings challenged.

Ethics for Performance Studies

Any consideration of performance ethics must move in three directions at the same time, addressing three interrelated issues: ethical pitfalls, traditional ethical models, and indigenous performance ethics connected to political theatre (Boal, 1995). Conquergood (1985, p. 4) has identified four ethical pitfalls that performance ethnographers must avoid: the custodian's rip-off, the enthusiast's infatuation, the skeptic's cop-out, and the curator's exhibitionism.

Cultural custodians, or cultural imperialists, ransack their biographical past looking for good texts to perform and then perform them for a fee, often denigrating a family member or a cultural group that regards such experiences as sacred. The enthusiast's infatuation, or superficial stance, occurs when the writer (and the performer) fail to become deeply involved in the cultural setting which they re-perform. Conquergood (1985, p. 6) says this trivializes the other because their experiences are neither contextualized nor well understood.

Modifying Conquergood (1985), the skeptic or cynic values detachment and being cynical. This position refuses to face up to the "ethical tensions and moral ambiguities of performing culturally sensitive materials" (p. 8). Finally, the curator or sensationalist, like the custodian, is a performer who sensationalizes the cultural differences that supposedly define the world of the other. He or she stages performances for the voyeur's gaze, perhaps telling stories about an abusive, hurtful other (p. 7).

These ethical stances make problematic the questions: How far into the other's world can the performer and the audience go? Of course we can never know the mind of another, only the other's performances. We can only know our own minds, and sometimes not well. This means that the differences that define the other's world must always be respected. There is no null point in the moral universe (Conquergood, 1985, pp. 8–9).

The second issue is implicit in Conquergood's four ethical pitfalls. He presumes a researcher who is held accountable to a set of universal ethical principles that are both duty-based and utilitarian. Duty-based ethics assume researchers and performers who are virtuous, have good intentions, and are committed to values like justice, honesty, and respect. This is Conquergood's ideal performer. However, Conquergood is concerned with more than good intentions; he is concerned with the effects, or consequences, of a performance on a person or a community. Thus he appears to implicitly endorse a utilitarian ethics based on consequences and pragmatic effects, not good intentions. This is the cost-benefit utilitarian model used by human subject review boards when they ask how this research will benefit society.

Both of these models have deficiencies. Carried to the extreme, the duty position can result in a moral absolutism, requiring that persons live up to an absolute standard, regardless of its human consequences (Edwards & Mauthner, 2002, p. 20; Kvale, 1996, pp. 121–122). But who holds these values? Whose values are they? The utilitarian model is predicated on the belief that the ends justify the means (Kvale, 1996, p. 122), thus the "wrongness or rightness of actions are judged by their consequences, not their intent" (Edwards & Mauthner, 2002, p. 20). Whose consequences are being considered? Whose means are being used, best for whom?

It is necessary to contrast these two universalist models with feminist and critical pedagogically informed ethical models (Edwards & Mauthner, 2002, p. 21). Contingent feminist ethical models work outward from personal experience and from local systems of meaning and truth, to social contexts where experience is shaped by nurturing social relationships based on care, respect, and love. The researcher is an insider to the group, not an outsider (Smith, 1999, p. 139). The desire is to enact a locally situated, contingent, feminist, communitarian ethic that respects and protects the rights, interests, and sensitivities of those one is working with, including ideas specific to the cultural context (Denzin, 1997, p. 275; L. T. Smith, 2012, p. 124).

Contingent ethical models have been adopted by social science professional associations that often navigate between universal normative models and contingent ethical directives (Edwards & Mauthner, 2002, p. 21). Such guidelines are then meant to guide the researcher when the kinds of pitfalls and dilemmas Conquergood identifies are encountered.

These professional guidelines do not include a space for culturally specific ethical ideas and values. In specific contexts, for instance, the Maori, specific ethical values and rules are prescribed in cultural terms. These understandings include showing respect for others, listening, sharing, and being generous, cautious, and humble. Linda Smith (2012) is quite explicit: "From indigenous perspectives ethical codes of conduct serve partly the same purposes as the protocols which govern our relationships with each other and with the environment" (p. 25).

In contrast to social science codes of ethics and the protocols used by human subject review boards, critical pedagogy seeks to enact a situationally contingent ethic that is compatible with indigenous values. This ethic is predicated on a *pedagogy of hope.* It is based on values shared in the group. It blends intentions with consequences. It presumes that well-intended, trusting, honest, virtuous persons engage in moral acts that have positive consequences for others. This is a communitarian dialogical *ethic of care* and responsibility. It presumes that performances occur in sacred aesthetic spaces where *research* does not operate as a dirty word. It presumes that performers treat persons, their cares, and their concerns with dignity and respect. Indeed, the values that structure the performance are those shared by the community and its members. These values include care, trust, and reciprocity. Because of these shared understandings, this model assumes that there will be few ethical dilemmas requiring negotiation.

A feminist, communitarian performance ethic is utopian in vision. While criticizing systems of injustice and oppression, it imagines how things could be different. It enacts a *performance pedagogy of radical democratic hope.* "What African American minstrels created was a new form of theater based in the skills of the performers, not their ability to conform to stereotypes" (Bean, 2001, pp. 187–188).

An empowering performance pedagogy frames the third issue that must be addressed. The multivoiced performance text enacts a pedagogy of hope. A critical consciousness is invoked. The performance event engenders moral discernment that guides social transformation (Christians, 2000; Denzin, 2003, p. 112). The performance text is grounded in the cruelties and injustices of daily life. Like Boal's radical theater, a documentary-drama format may be used, drawing on current events and media accounts of these events. A radical performance ethic is grounded in a politics of resistance. The performance must be ethically honest. It must be dialogical, seeking to locate dialogue and meaningful exchange in the *radical center.*

The other always exists, as Trinh (1989) would argue, in the spaces on each side of the hyphen (Conquergood, 1985, p. 9). The performance text can only be dialogic, a text that does not speak about or for the other, but which "speaks to and with them" (Conquergood, 1985, p. 10). It is a text that reengages the past and brings it alive in the present. The dialogic text attempts to keep the dialogue, the conversation—between text, the past, the present, performer, and audience—ongoing and open-ended (Conquergood, 1985, p. 9). This text does more than invoke empathy; it interrogates, criticizes, and empowers. This is dialogical criticism. The dialogical performance is the means for "honest intercultural understanding" (Conquergood, 1985, p. 10).

If this understanding is to be created, the following elements need to be present. Scholars must have the energy, imagination, courage, and commitment to create these texts (see Conquergood, 1985, p. 10). Audiences must be drawn to the sites where these performances take place, and they must be willing to suspend normal aesthetic frameworks so that coparticipatory performances can be produced. Boal (1995) is clear on this: "In the Theatre of the Oppressed we try to . . . make the dialogue between stage and audience totally transitive" (p. 42). In these sites a shared field of emotional experience is created, and in these moments of sharing, critical cultural awareness is awakened.

Critical pedagogical theater creates dialogical performances that follow these directives from Boal (1995, p. 42):

1. Every oppressed person is a subjugated subversive.

2. The cop in our head represents our submission to this oppression.

3. Each person possesses the ability to be subversive.

4. Critical pedagogical theater can empower persons to be subversive while making their submission to oppression disappear.

The co-performed text aims to enact a feminist, communitarian moral ethic. This ethic presumes a dialogical view of the self and its performances. It seeks narratives that ennoble human experience, performances that facilitate civic transformations in the public and private spheres. This ethic ratifies the dignities of the self and honors personal struggle. It understands cultural criticism to be a form of empowerment, arguing that empowerment begins in that ethical moment when individuals are lead into the troubling spaces occupied by others. In the moment of co-performance, lives are joined and struggle begins anew.

Ethical Injunctions

Does this performance . . .

- Nurture critical (race) consciousness?
- Use historical restagings and traditional texts to subvert and critique official ideology?
- Heal? Empower?
- Avoid Conquergood's four pitfalls?

- Enact a feminist, communitarian, socially contingent ethic?
- Present a pedagogy of hope?

The critical imagination is radically democratic, pedagogical, and interventionist. This imagination dialogically inserts itself into the world, provoking conflict, curiosity, criticism, and reflection. Extending Freire (1998), performance autoethnography contributes to a conception of education and democracy as pedagogies of freedom. As praxis, performance ethnography is a way of acting on the world in order to change it.

The Politics of Interpretation

Writing, Richardson (2001, p. 879) asserts, is not an innocent practice, although in the social sciences and the humanities there is only interpretation. Nonetheless Marx (1983, p. 158) continues to remind us that we are in the business of not just interpreting but changing the world.

Qualitative researchers who write interpretive texts have four lessons to learn from the recent poststructural, postmodern turns in qualitative inquiry. Each lesson involves the social text and the study of lived experience.

First, the worlds we study are created through the texts we write. We do not study lived experience; we study (and create) lived textuality. Experience is always mediated and shaped by prior textual and cultural understandings which are then re-inscribed in the social text.

Second, the social text is a performance, performative writing, a visual construction, a re-representation of the dialogue, voice, and actions of the other. Through the lens of the text, the reader confronts the other whose partial presence is given in quotes and excerpts from talk. These visual representations and performances of voice and presence are textual constructions, specular displays of the other's lived textuality.

Third, there is no external authority for these textual representations. Their legitimation cannot be given by invoking a reality that lies outside the text. Traditionally the province of validity, a text's legitimacy has been grounded in its connection to what is observed, measured, or investigated. These external realities confer or withhold various honors for the text. It has, for example, high or low versions of construct, external, internal, instrumental, pragmatic, predictive, concurrent, face, apparent, or consensual validity. Or its findings are trustworthy, credible, dependable, confirmable, and transferable. Validity, a text's claim to authority, can only be given internally, by the claims and spaces it makes and offers to the reader.

Fourth, the authority of a text rests on an experiential structure that moves in three directions at the same time. The text must reach out from the writer to the world studied. It must articulate a set of self-referential experiences that allow the writer to make sense of and understand this world in moral and political terms. And the text must speak back to the world it describes.

The intention, with each of these textual moves, is not to convince the reader, the writer, or the other that this interpretation constitutes the most valid or correct version of the Truth. Understanding is desired: the guiding question is simple: Have I as a writer created an experiential text that allows me (and you) to understand what I have studied? Understanding occurs when you (and I) are able to interpret what has been described within a framework that is subjectively, emotionally, and causally meaningful. This is the verisimilitude of the experiential text, a text that does not map or attempt to reproduce the real.

The goal is the production of a text that creates its own conditions of understanding. This form of verisimilitude is textual. This text rests on that version of the world I have entered and studied. It articulates the emotional, moral, and political meanings this world has for me. It works outward from my biography to a body of experiences that have made a difference in my life and hopefully in the lives of others.

Such texts move readers and writers to action. They mark and re-inscribe passing epiphanic experience and give it meaning, allowing others to vicariously share in that experience. They re-anchor the text in its historical moment and define the writer as a storyteller who has something important to say about this moment and its personal and public troubles. Experientially grounded, these texts speak alongside the voices of science, privileging the personal over the institutional. So conceived, this form of textuality challenges empirical science's hegemonic control over qualitative inquiry. Refusing the identity of empirical science, the experiential text becomes a form of social criticism that no longer seeks validation in scientific discourse.

In the next chapter I briefly discuss the problem of representing lives.

Notes

1. This chapter reworks material in Denzin (2009, pp. 151–173).

2. These narratives enact Turner's (1986b) four-fold processual model of breach, crisis, redress, reintegration or schism.

3. Definitions: *aesthetics:* theories of beauty; *ethics:* theories of ought, of right; *epistemology:* theories of knowing; *anti-aesthetic:* denies a privileged aesthetic realm, is political. I seek a radical anti-aesthetic that operates as political critique, challenging at every turn the aestheticization of everyday life and modernist ethical models.

4. I thank Clifford Christians for clarifying these principles.

5. She uses the term *research poetry* to reference "poems that are crafted from research endeavors" (Faulkner, 2009, p. 20), work that turns interviews, transcripts, observations, and personal experience into poetic form.

6 In Conclusion: Performing Lives

Autoethnography works this territory between the orienting and disorienting story. (Gingrich-Philbrook, 2013, p. 609)

In Praise of the Poetic

Laurel Richardson's (1992, 1997) poem "Louisa May's Story of Her Life" provides a perfect example of how the poetic performance turn can work. The performance text was created from the transcription of an in-depth interview Richardson had conducted with Louisa May, an unwed mother. In the text Richardson used only Louisa May's words and syntax. Here is an extract

> The most important thing
>
> To say . . . is that
>
> I grew up in the South.
>
> Being southern shapes
>
> Aspirations . . . shapes
>
> What you think you're going to be . . .
>
> I grew up poor in a rented house. (Richardson, 1992, p. 20)

Richardson stated that she wanted a framework and a method that went beyond sociological naturalism, beyond positivistic commitments to tell an objective story. She wanted to use literary and poetical devices like repetition, pauses, meter, rhymes, diction, and tone to write Louisa May's life (Richardson, 1992; 1997, pp. 142–143).

She transcribed Louisa May's interview into 36 pages of prose text. She then shaped it into a performance narrative.

What possessed me to do so was head wrestling with postmodern issues about the nature of "data," the interview as an international event, the representation of lives. The core problems raised by postmodernism—voice, presence, subjectivity, the politics of evidence, the inability of transcripts to capture reflexive experience—seemed resolvable through the poetic form which re-creates embodied speech. (Richardson, 1992, p. 23; 1997, p. 143)

In moving from interview to the transcribed text, to the poetic representation, Richardson kept the pauses, the line breaks, the spaces within and between lines, the places where to be quiet, when to be loud.

When performed, the poetic representation opens up to multiple open-ended readings, in the ways that straight sociological prose does not permit. This writing-performance text is reflexive and alive (Richardson, 1992, p. 25; 1997, pp. 142–143; Richardson & St. Pierre, 2005, p. 964). It is never transparent. It has to be read, performed. Thus does Richardson show how she did her work, noting, too, that she worked carefully with her wiring group as she moved from one step to the next in the production of this work.

The poetic representation of lives is never just an end in itself. The goal is political, to change the way we think about people and their lives and to use the poetic-performative format to do this. The poet makes the world visible in new and different ways, in ways ordinary social science writing does not allow. The poet is accessible, visible, and present in the text, in ways that traditional writing forms discourage.

At this level, It is obvious that all the forms of creative, analytic, interpretive practice outlined by Richardson and St. Pierre (2005, p. 962) need to be honored:

Performance writing,

autoethnography,

literary and ethnographic fiction,

poetry

ethnodrama,

writing stories,

reader's theatre,

layered texts,

aphorisms,

conversations, epistles, memoirs,

polyvocal texts,

comedy, satire, allegory

visual and multi-media texts,

dense theory,

museum displays,

dance,

choreographed findings

These performance texts are always:

political,

emotional,

analytic,

interpretive,

pedagogical,

local, partial,

incomplete,

painful to

read,

exhilarating.

It seems fitting to end with obituaries, for, in these endings, surely the final meanings of a person's life are found.

Obituaries

Here is how the *New York Times* (July 20, 1988, p. 50) reported the death of Martin J. Walsh:

Martin J. Walsh
Actor, 41

New York, July 19—Martin J. Walsh, an actor, died of acquired immune deficiency syndrome on July 7 at New York University Medical Center in Manhattan. He was 41 years old.

Mr. Walsh appeared in Broadway in "The Pirates of Penzance" and "Shenandoah" and many other Off Broadway productions. He was a member of the Prince Street Players, a children's theater company, in the 1970s.
He is survived by his father ... a brother ... and three sisters.

The small number of lines given to Mr. Walsh and his death contrasts with the three-column story, accompanied by a photograph, of Raymond Carver's death, reported in the same newspaper on Wednesday, August 3, 1988.

Like Mr. Walsh's life and death, Mr. Carver's life is recorded in terms of his work and the family he left behind. But Mr. Carver's biography is filled out. He is called a writer and poet of the working poor. Frog, his childhood nickname, is discussed, as are his collections of short stories, the awards he won, his early childhood, his marriages, his alcoholism, his divorce from his first wife, his operations for cancer, his relation to the poet Tess Gallagher, and his final moments alive on his porch looking at his rose garden while he talked about Chekov's death.

The obituary makes a public statement of a life's end. It represents a narrative form which goes from birth (the beginning) to death (the end). It gives a life a finite temporal space. It then fills out that space with the accomplishments of the person. It makes a life consubstantial with its achievements. When, as in the case of Mr. Carver, the life that was led was noteworthy, then personal words and personal experience stories from the dead individual's life are recorded. Unnoteworthy lives seldom get such coverage.

Are we to assume that Martin J. Walsh's life was any less significant than Raymond Carver's because less space was devoted to it? Surely not for his father, brother, and three sisters. Both men suffered from diseases: Walsh died from his, AIDS; Carver presumably recovered from his alcoholism. Both of these social diseases became part of the public biographies in their moment of death. The obituary seeks a cause for life's end, and it attempts to find in that cause an interpretation of the life that died from it. Whether the cause is AIDS, cancer, alcoholism, or old age, that cause, a marker of an ending, is read back into a life, showing that one final meaning of a life is always given in terms of its ending.

But even this search for final causes is itself open-ended, for the life that is inscribed in the obituary is presented as an ongoing concern. Mr. Walsh's life goes on in the memories of his family, and Mr. Carver's life is similarly continued in his obituary; he, like Mr. Walsh, lives on in his works. The obituary, then, is never a closed text, even though it presents itself as being one.

The obituary treats each individual as a universal singular, and in this literary move, it recognizes that each individual's life is itself a singular accomplishment which demands recognition. That achievement, summed up in the activities and experiences of the person, is all that the person is or ever was. This named entity, this person who is dead, is now brought before us in full biographical garb. Here in these bare details we find that all a life is, as far as the public is concerned, is what its owner did and who he or she leaves behind. A life, like the stories that can be told about it, never ends. But there is more, and Gary, whom we met in Chapter 4, tells us this in his private self-narrative. There is a deep, inner self groping for meaning, and this self and its meanings are forever and always unfinished productions. The biographical interpretive method is always incomplete, for the lives and experiences this method attempts to represent are themselves never done. Newspapers can't allow this, nor can sociologists. But some everyday, ordinary people and the people who write about them—like Raymond Carver—do.

Final Performances

Stewart (2013, p. 661) reminds us that when a life ends it's as if it bursts, leaving wet weights all over the landscape. The living live in a state of dispersal.

> What happened to her toothbrush?
>   Where are the little pearl earrings she wore through the long duration of a decade of life in the process of losing itself one quality at a time?
>   The line between self and other, subject and object, person and event, is smeared, rubbed out like a child's crayon experiment. The distinctions between things are flooded by unspeakable dullness of sheer loss. . . .
>   Your eyes try to dwell in the scene of the last time you touched her. She was blind, paralyzed, deaf. Her fingers would walk down her starving body to find your hand. . . .
>   They say there are stages to grief. . . . It's time to say goodbye. (Stewart, 2013, pp. 661–663)

Performance autoethnography allows us to bring the world into play, to make it visible, to bring it alive and "exposed on the stage of the world" (Lopate, 1997, p. 50; also Stewart, 2013, p. 667). And it allows me to do more. It allows me, in fits of nostalgia, to forge a link between myself and the world, the living and the dead, a reaching out to "what seems to be slipping away, or transmogrifying into something harsh and loud" (Stewart, 2013, p. 660). It allows me to make fleeting sense out of a world gone mad, and I need this because "the world does not make very much sense to me right now" (Gingrich-Philbrook, 2013, p. 609).

References

Adams, T. E. (2011). *Narrating the closet: An autoethnography of same-sex attraction.* Walnut Creek, CA: Left Coast Press.

Adams, T. E., & Jones, S. H. (2008). Autoethnography is queer. In N. K. Denzin, Y. S. Lincoln, & L. T. Smith (Eds.), *Handbook of critical and indigenous methodologies* (pp. 373–390). Thousand Oaks, CA: Sage.

Adams, T., Jones, S. H., & Ellis, C. (2013). Conclusion: Storying our future. In S. H. Jones, T. E. Adams, C. Ellis (Eds.), *Handbook of autoethnography* (pp. 669–677). Walnut Creek, CA: Left Coast Press.

Alcoholics Anonymous. (1976). *Alcoholics Anonymous: The story of how many thousands of men and women have recovered from alcoholism* (3rd ed.). New York: Alcoholics Anonymous.

Alexander, B. K. 2000. Skin flint (or, the garbage man's kid): A generative autobiographical performance based on Tami Spry's tattoo stories. *Text and Performance Quarterly, 20,* 97–114.

Anderson, L. (2006). Analytic autoethnography. *Journal of Contemporary Ethnography, 35,* 373–395.

Barthes, R. (1985). *The grain of the voice: Interviews: 1962–1980* (L. Coverdale, Trans.). New York, NY: Hill & Wang.

Bean, A. (2001). Black minstrelsy and double inversion, circa 1890. In H. J. Elam Jr. & D. Krasner (Eds.), *African American performance and theatre history* (pp. 171–191). New York, NY: Oxford University Press.

Becker, H. S. (1986). *Doing things together: Selected papers.* Evanston, IL: Northwestern University Press.

Bertaux, D, (Ed.). (1981). *Biography and society: The Life history approach in the social sciences.* Beverly Hills, CA: Sage.

Bertaux, D. (1987). Review essay of "L'illusion biographique" by Pierre Bourdieu. *Life Stories/Récits de Vie, 3,* 47–50.

Bertaux, D., & Kohli, M. (1984). The life story approach: A continental view. *Annual Review of Sociology, 10,* 215–237.

Birringer, J. (1993). *Theatre, theory, postmodernism.* Bloomington: Indiana University Press.

Boal, A. (1995). *The rainbow of desire: The Boal method of theatre and therapy.* London, UK: Routledge.

Bochner, A. P. (2000). Criteria against ourselves. *Qualitative Inquiry, 5,* 266–272.

Bochner, A. P., & Riggs, N. (in press). Producing narrative inquiry. In P. Leavy (Ed.),. *Handbook of qualitative methods.* New York, NY: Oxford University Press.

Bourdieu, P. (1986). L'illusion biographique. *Acts de la Recherche en Sciences Sociales, 62/63,* 69–72.

Bruner, E. M. (1986). Experience and its expressions. In V. M. Turner & E. M. Bruner (Eds.), *The anthropology of experience* (pp. 3–30). Urbana: University of Illinois Press.

Burke, J. L. (2009). *Rain gods.* New York, NY: Simon & Schuster.

Butler, J. (1993). *Bodies that matter.* New York, NY: Routledge.

Butler, J. (1995). For a careful reading. In S. Benhabib, J. Butler, D. Cornell, & N. Fraser (Eds.), *Feminist contentions: A philosophical exchange* (pp. 127–143). New York, NY: Routledge.

Catlin, G. (1848). *Catlin's notes of eight years' travels and residence in Europe, with his North American Indian collection, with anecdotes and incidents of the travels and adventures of three different parties of American Indians whom he introduced to the courts of England, France, and Belgium, in two volumes. Vol. I.* London, England: Author.

Chang, H., Ngunjiri, F. W., & Hernandez, K.-A. C. (2013). *Collaborative autoethnography.* Walnut Creek, CA: Left Coast Press.

Christians, C. (2000). Ethics and politics in qualitative research. In N. K. Denzin & Y. S. Lincoln (Eds.), *Handbook of qualitative research* (2nd ed., pp. 133–155). Thousand Oaks, CA: Sage.

Clifford, J., & Marcus, G. (Eds.). (1986). *Writing culture: The poetics and politics of ethnography.* Berkeley: University of California Press.

Clough, P. T. (1988). *Women Writing and the Life History: A Reading of Toni Morrison's The Bluest Eye.* (Unpublished manuscript)

Clough, P. T. (1990). The Deconstruction of ethnographic subjectivity and the construction of deliberate belief. *Studies in Symbolic Interaction, 11,* 35-44.

Clough, P. T. (2000). Comments on setting criteria for experimental writing. *Qualitative Inquiry, 6,* 278–291.

Clough, P. T. (2007). Introduction, In P. T. Clough & J. Halley (Eds.), *The affective turn: Theorizing the social* (pp. 1–33). Durham, NC: Duke University Press.

Cohn, R. (1988). Realism. In M. Banham (Ed.), *The Cambridge guide to theatre* (p. 815). Cambridge, UK: Cambridge University Press.

Collins, P. H. (1991). *Black feminist thought.* New York, NY: Routledge.

Conquergood, D. (1985). Performing as a moral act: Ethical dimensions of the ethnography of performance. *Literature in Performance, 5*(1), 1–13.

Conquergood, D. (1998). Beyond the text: Toward a performative cultural politics. In S. J. Dailey (Ed.), *The future of performance studies: Visions and revisions* (pp. 25–36). Annandale, VA: National Communication Association.

Davies, B. (2006). Collective biography as ethically reflexive practice. In B. Davies & S. Gannon (Eds.), *Doing collective biography: Investigating the production of subjectivity* (pp. 182–189). Maidenhead, UK: Open University Press.

Davies, B., & Gannon, S. (2006). Prologue. In B. Davies & S. Gannon (Eds.), *Doing collective biography: Investigating the production of subjectivity* (pp. iv–x). Maidenhead, UK: Open University Press.

Deloria, V., Jr. (1969). *Custer died for your sins: An Indian manifesto.* Norman: University of Oklahoma Press.

Deloria, V., Jr. (1997). Vine Deloria, Native American author and teacher. In S. Terkel (Ed.), *The Studs Terkel reader: My American century* (pp. 34–38). New York, NY: New Press.

Denzin, N. K. (1984). *On understanding emotion.* San Francisco, CA: Jossey-Bass.

Denzin, N. K. (1986). Interpretive interactionism and the use of life stories. *Revista Internacional de Sociologia, 44,* 321–339.

Denzin, N. K. (1987). *The recovering alcoholic.* Newbury Park, CA: Sage.

Denzin, N. K. (1997). *Interpretive ethnography: Ethnographic practices for the 21st century.* Thousand Oaks, CA: Sage.

Denzin, N. K. (2001). *Interpretive interactionism* (2nd ed.). Newbury Park, CA: Sage.

Denzin, N. K. (2003). *Performance ethnography: Critical pedagogy and the politics of culture.* Thousand Oaks, CA: Sage.

Denzin, N. K. (2005). Indians in the park. *Qualitative Research, 3,* 9–33.

Denzin, N. K. (2008). *Searching for Yellowstone: Performing race, nation and nature in the new west.* Walnut Creek, CA: Left Coast Press.

Denzin, N. K. (2009). *Qualitative inquiry under fire.* Walnut Creek, CA: Left Coast Press.

Denzin, N. K. (2010). *The qualitative manifesto: A call to arms.* Walnut Creek, CA: Left Coast Press.

Denzin, N. K. (2011). *Custer on canvas: Representing Indians, memory and violence in the new west.* Walnut Creek, CA: Left Coast Press.

Denzin, N. K. (2013a). *Indians on display: Global commodification of Native America in performance, art, and museums.* Walnut Creek, CA: Left Coast Press.

Denzin, N. K. (2013b). Interpretive autoethnography. In S. H. Jones, T. E. Adams, & C. Ellis (Eds.), *Handbook of autoethnography* (pp. 123–142). Walnut Creek, CA: Left Coast Press.

Derrida, J. (1973). *Speech and phenomena.* Evanston, IL: Northwestern University Press. (Original work published 1967)

Derrida, J. (1972). Structure, Sign and Play in the Discourse of the Human Sciences, In R. Macksey & E. Donato (Eds.), *The structuralist controversy: The languages of criticism and the sciences of man* (pp. 247–265). Baltimore, MD: Johns Hopkins University Press.

Derrida, J. (1981). *Positions.* Chicago, IL: University of Chicago Press. (Original work published 1972)

Diversi, M., & Moreira, C. (2009). *Betweener talk: Decolonizing knowledge production, pedagogy, and praxis.* Walnut Creek, CA: Left Coast Press.

Dylan, B. (2004). *Chronicles, Vol. 1.* New York, NY: Simon & Schuster.

Edwards, R., & Mauthner, M. (2002). Ethics and feminist research: Theory and practice. In M. Mauthner, M. Birch, J. Jessop, & T. Miller (Eds.), *Ethics in qualitative research* (pp. 14–31). London, UK: Sage.

Ellis, C. (2000). Creating criteria: An autoethnographic story. *Qualitative Inquiry, 5,* 273–277.

Ellis, C. (2009). *Revision: Autoethnographic reflections on life and work.* Walnut Creek, CA: Left Coast Press.

Ellis, C. (2013). Preface: Carrying the torch for autoethnography. In S. H. Jones, T. E. Adams, C. Ellis (Eds.), *Handbook of autoethnography* (pp. xx–xx). Walnut Creek, CA: Left Coast Press.

Ellis, C., Adams, T. E., & Bochner, A. P. (2011). Autoethnography: An overview. *Forum: Qualitative Social Research, 12*(1), 1–14.

Ellis, C., & Bochner, A. P. (2000). Autoethnography, personal narrative, reflexivity: Researcher as subject. In N. K. Denzin & Y. S. Lincoln (Eds.), *Handbook of qualitative research* (2nd ed., pp. 733–768). Thousand Oaks, CA: Sage.

Faulkner, S. L. (2009). *Poetry as method: Reporting research through verse.* Walnut Creek, CA: Left Coast Press.

Feibleman, P. (1988). *Lilly: Reminiscences of Lillian Hellman.* New York, NY: William Morrow.

Gale, K., Pelias, R., Russell, L., Spry, T., & Wyatt, J. (2013). Intensity: A collaborative autoethnography. *International Review of Qualitative Research, 6*(1), 165–180.

Gale, K., & Wyatt, J. (2009). *Between the two: A nomadic inquiry into collaborative writing and subjectivity.* Newcastle Upon Tyne, UK: Cambridge Scholars.

Garoian, C. R. (1999). *Performing pedagogy: Toward an art of politics.* Albany: State University of New York Press.

Garoian, C. R., & Gaudelius, Y. M. (2008). *Spectacle pedagogy: Art, politics, and visual culture.* Albany: State University of New York Press.

Geertz, C. (1973). *Interpreting cultures.* New York: Basic Books.

Geertz, C. (1988). *Works and lives: The anthropologist as author.* Stanford, CA: Stanford University Press.

Gilroy, P. (1991). *There ain't no Black in the Union Jack: The cultural politics of race and nation.* Chicago, IL: University of Chicago Press.

Gingrich-Philbrook, C. (2013). Evaluating (evaluations of) autoethnography. In S. H. Jones, T. E. Adams, & C. Ellis (Eds.), *Handbook of autoethnography* (pp. 609–626). Walnut Creek, CA: Left Coast Press.

Giroux, H. (2001). *Cultural studies as performative politics.* Cultural Studies–Critical Methodlogies, 1, 5–23.

Glaser, B. G., & Strauss, A. L. (1967). *The discovery of grounded theory.* Chicago: Aldine.

Goffman, E. (1959). *The presentation of self in everyday life.* New York, NY: Doubleday.

Goodall, H. L., Jr. (2012). Three cancer poems. *Qualitative Inquiry, 18,* 724–727.

Gorman, G. (2012). Divorce: The aftermath. *Qualitative Inquiry, 18,* 843–844.

Halley, J. O. (2012). *The parallel lives of women and cows.* New York, NY: Palgrave.

Hamera, J. (2011). Performance ethnography. In N. K. Denzin & Y. Lincoln (Eds.), *Handbook of qualitative research* (4th ed., pp. 317–330). Thousand Oaks, CA: Sage.

Hanauer, D. I. (2012). Growing up in the unseen shadow of the Kindertransport: A poetic-narrative autoethnography. *Qualitative Inquiry, 18,* 845–851.

Heidegger, M. (1962). *Being and time.* New York, NY: Harper and Row.

Hellman, L. (1970). *An unfinished woman.* Boston, MA: Little, Brown.

Hellman, L. (1973). *Pentimento.* Boston, MA: Little, Brown.

Hellman, L. (1976). *Scoundrel time.* Boston, MA: Little, Brown.

hooks, b. (1990). *Yearning: Race, gender and cultural politics.* Boston, MA: South End Press.

Hutchinson, L. D. (1981). *Anna J. Cooper.* Washington, DC: Smithsonian Institution Press.

Jackson, A. Y., & Mazzei, L. A. (Eds.). (2009). *Voice in qualitative inquiry: Challenging conventional, interpretive, and critical conceptions in qualitative research*, London, UK: Routledge.

Jackson, A. Y., Mazzei, L. A. (2012). *Thinking with theory in qualitative research: Viewing data across multiple perspectives.* London, UK: Routledge.

Jameson, F.. (1990). *Signatures of the visible.* New York, NY: Routledge.

Jones, S. H. (2013). The performance space: Giving an account of performance studies. *Text and Performance Quarterly, 33*(1), 77–80.

Jones, S. H., Adams, T. E., & Ellis, C. (2013a). Coming to know autoethnography as more than a method. In S. H. Jones, T. E. Adams, C. Ellis (Eds.), *Handbook of autoethnography.* Walnut Creek, CA: Left Coast Press.

Jones, S. H., Adams, T. E., & Ellis, C. (Eds.). (2013b). *Handbook of autoethnography.* Walnut Creek, CA: Left Coast Press.

Kanfer, S. (1988, September 11). Review of *Lilly: Reminiscences of Lillian Hellman* by Peter Feibleman. *New York Times Book Review,* pp. 15–16, 18.

Kvale, S. (1996). *InterViews: An introduction to qualitative research interviewing.* London, UK: Sage.

Lather, P. (2009). Against empathy, voice and authenticity. In A. Y. Jackson & L. A. Mazzei (Eds.), *Voice in qualitative inquiry: Challenging conventional, interpretive and critical conceptions in qualitative research* (pp. 17–26). New York, NY: Routledge.

Lincoln, Y. S. (2002). Grief in an Appalachian register. *Qualitative Inquiry, 8,* 146–149.

Lockford, L. (1998). Emergent issues in the performance of a border-transgressive narrative. In S. J. Dailey (Ed.), *The future of performance studies: Visions and revisions* (pp. 214–220). Annandale, VA: National Communication Association.

Lopate, P. (1997). *The art of the personal essay.* New York, NY: Anchor Press.

MacLure, M. (2011). Qualitative inquiry: Where are the ruins? *Qualitative Inquiry, 17,* 997–1005.

MacLure, M. (2012, October 5). The Death of Data? [Web log post]. Retrieved from http://www.esriblog.info/the-death-of-data

MacLure, M. (2013). Classification or wonder? Coding as an analytic practice in qualitative research. In R. Coleman & J. Ringrose (Eds.), *Deleuze and research methodologies* (pp. 164–183). Edinburgh, Scotland: Edinburgh University Press.

Madison, D. S. (1998). Performances, personal narratives, and the politics of possibility. In S. J. Dailey (Ed.), *The future of performance studies: Visions and revisions* (pp. 276–286). Annandale, VA: National Communication Association.

Madison, D. S. (2005). *Critical ethnography.* Thousand Oaks, CA: Sage.

Madison, D. S. (2010). *Acts of activism: Human rights as radical performance.* Cambridge, UK: Cambridge University Press.

Madison, D. S. (2012). *Critical ethnography* (2nd ed.). Thousand Oaks, CA: Sage.

Martin J. Walsh, Actor, 41. (1988, July 20). *New York Times,* p. 50.

Marx, K. (1983) From the eighteenth Brumaire of Louis Bonaparte. In E. Kamenka (Ed.), *The portable Karl Marx* (pp. 287–323). New York, NY: Penguin. (Original work published 1852)

Mazzei, L. A., & Jackson, A. Y. (2009). Introduction: The limit of voice. In A. Y. Jackson & L. A. Mazzei (Eds.), *Voice in qualitative inquiry: Challenging conventional, interpretive and critical conceptions in qualitative research* (pp. 1–13). New York, NY: Routledge.

McCall, M. (1985). Life history and social change. *Studies in Symbolic Interaction, 6*, 169–182.

McCall, M. (1989). The significance of storytelling. *Studies in Symbolic Interaction, 11*, 145–161.

McCall, M., & Wittner, J. (1988, April). *The good news about life history.* Paper presented to the Annual Symposium of the Society for the Study of Symbolic Interaction, Chicago, IL.

Mills, C. W. (1959). *The sociological imagination.* New York, NY: Oxford University Press.

Minge, J. M., & Zimmerman, A. L. (2013). *Concrete and dust: Mapping the sexual terrains of Los Angeles.* New York, NY: Routledge.

Misch, G. (1951). *A history of autobiography in antiquity, Vol. I.* Cambridge, MA: Harvard University Press.

Montaigne, M. de. (1958). *The complete essays of Montaigne* (D. M. Frame, Trans.). Stanford, CA: Stanford University Press. (Original work published 1572–1588)

Moreira, C. (2012). I hate chicken breast: A tale of resisting stories and disembodied knowledge construction. *International Journal of Qualitative Studies in Education, 25*(2), 151–167.

Norris, J., & Sawyer, R. D. (2012). Toward a dialogic methodology. In J. Norris, R. D. Sawyer, D. E. Lund (Eds.), *Duoethnography: Dialogic methods for social health and educational research* (pp. 9–39). Walnut Creek, CA: Left Coast Press.

Panourgia, N., & Marcus, G. E. (Eds.). (2008). *Ethnographica moralia: Experiments in interpretive anthropology.* New York, NY: Fordham University Press.

Pelias, R. J. (1999). *Writing performance: Poeticizing the researcher's body.* Carbondale: Southern Illinois University.

Pelias, R. J. (2004). *A methodology of the heart.* Walnut Creek, CA: AltaMira Press.

Pelias, R. J. (2011). *Leaning: A poetics of personal relations.* Walnut Creek, CA: Left Coast Press.

Pinar, W. (1975). Currere: Toward reconceptualization. In W. Pinar (Ed.), *Curriculum theorizing: The reconceptualists* (pp. 396–414). Berkeley, CA: McCutchan.

Plath, D. W. (1987). Making experience come out right: Culture as biography. *Central Issues in Anthropology, 7*, 1–8.

Pollock, D. (1998a). Introduction: Making history go. In D. Pollock (Ed.), *Exceptional spaces: Essays in performance and history* (pp. 1–45). Chapel Hill: University of North Carolina Press.

Pollock, D. (1998b). Performing Writing. In P. Phelan & J. Lane (Eds.), *The ends of performance* (pp. 73–193). New York, NY: New York University Press.

Pollock, D. (1998c). A response to Dwight Conquergood's essay "Beyond the text: Towards a performative cultural politics." In S. J. Dailey (Ed.), *The future of performance studies: Visions and revisions* (pp. 25–36). Annandale, VA: National Communication Association.

Pollock, D. (2007). The performative "I." *Cultural Studies—Critical Methodologies, 7*(3), 239–255.

Pollock, D. (2009). Beyond experience. *Cultural Studies—Critical Methodologies, 9*, 636–646.

Poulos, C. N. (2009). *Accidental ethnography.* Walnut Creek, CA: Left Coast Press.

Reed-Danahay, D. E. (1997). Introduction. In D. E. Reed-Danahay (Ed.), *Auto/ ethnography: Rewriting the self and the social* (pp. 1–20). New York, NY: Oxford University Press.

Richardson, L. (1992). The poetic representation of lives: Writing a postmodernist sociology. *Studies in Symbolic Interaction, 13,* 19–27.

Richardson, L. (1997). *Fields of play: Constructing an academic life.* New Brunswick, NJ: Rutgers University Press.

Richardson, L. (2000a). Evaluating Ethnography. *Qualitative Inquiry, 6,* 253–255.

Richardson, L. (2000b). Writing: A method of inquiry. In N. K. Denzin & Y. S. Lincoln (Eds.), *Handbook of qualitative research* (2nd ed., pp. 923–948) Thousand Oaks, CA: Sage.

Richardson, L. (2001). Poetic representation of interviews. In J. F. Gubrium & J. A. Holstein (Eds.), *Handbook of interview research* (pp. 877–892). Thousand Oaks, CA: Sage.

Richardson, L., & St. Pierre, E. A. (2005). Writing: A method of inquiry. In N. K. Denzin & Y. S. Lincoln (Eds.), *Handbook of qualitative research* (3rd ed., pp. 959–978). Thousand Oaks, CA: Sage.

Rollyson, C. (1988). *Lillian Hellman: Her legacy and her legend.* New York, NY: St. Martin's Press.

Roos, J. P. (1987). From farm to office: Family, self-confidence and the new middle class. *Life Stories/Récits de Vie, 3,* 7–20.

Rusted, B. (2006). Performing visual discourse: Cowboy art and institutional practice. *Text and Performance Quarterly, 26*(2), 115–137.

Saldana, J. (2005). An introduction to ethnodrama. In J. Saldana (Ed.), *Ethnodrama: An anthology of reality theatre* (pp. 1–36). Walnut Creek, CA: Left Coast Press.

Saldana, J. (2011). *Ethnotheatre: Research from page to stage.* Walnut Creek, CA: Left Coast Press.

Sartre, J.-P. (1952/1963). *Saint Genet: Actor and martyr.* New York: Pantheon.

Sartre, J.-P. (1963). *Search for a method.* New York, NY: Knopf.

Sartre, J.-P. (1981). *The family idiot: Gustave Flaubert, Volume 1, 1821–1857.* Chicago, IL: University of Chicago Press. (Original work published 1971)

Schechner, R. (1988). *Performance theory* (Rev. and expanded edition). New York, NY: Routledge.

Scott, J. (1991). The evidence of experience. *Critical Inquiry, 17,* 773–797.

Scott, J. (1992). Experience. In J. Butler & J. W. Scott (Eds.), *Feminists theorize the political* (pp. 22–40). New York, NY: Routledge.

Scott, J. (1993). The evidence of experience. In H. Ablelove, M. A. Barale, & J. Lane (Eds.), *The lesbian and gay studies reader* (pp. 397–415). New York, NY: Routlege.

Smith, D. E. (1990a). *The conceptual practices of power: A feminist sociology of knowledge.* Boston, MA: Northeastern University Press.

Smith, D. E. (1990b). *Texts, facts, and femininity: Exploring the relations of ruling.* New York, NY: Routledge.

Smith, L. T. (2012). *Decolonizing methodologies: Research and indigenous peoples* (2nd ed.). London, UK: Zed Books.

Spry, T. (2001). Performing autoethnography: An embodied methodological praxis. *Qualitative Inquiry, 7,* 706–732.

Spry, T. (2006). A "performative-I" co-presence: Embodying the ethnographic turn in performance and the performative turn in ethnography. *Text and Performance Quarterly, 26,* 339–346.

Spry, T. (2011). *Body, paper, stage: Writing and performing autoethnography.* Walnut Creek, CA: Left Coast Press.

Spry, T. (2013). Unseating the myth of a girl and her horse, now that's true grit. *Cultural Studies—Critical Methodologies, 12,* 482–484.

St. Pierre, E. A. (2009). Afterword: Decentering voice in qualitative inquiry. In A. Y. Jackson & L. A. Mazzei (Eds.), *Voice in qualitative inquiry: Challenging conventional, interpretive, and critical conceptions in qualitative research* (pp. 221–236). New York, NY: Routledge.

St. Pierre, E. A., & Pillow, W. (Eds.). (2000). *Working the ruins: Feminist poststructural methods in education.* New York, NY: Routledge.

Stake, R. (1994). Case studies. In N. K. Denzin & Y. S. Lincoln (Eds.), *Handbook of qualitative research* (pp. 236–247). Thousand Oaks, CA: Sage.

Stein, G. (1933). *The autobiography of Alice B. Toklas.* New York, NY: Harcourt, Brace.

Stewart, K. (2013). An autoethnography of what happens. In S. H. Jones, T. E. Adams, & C. Ellis (Eds.), *Handbook of autoethnography* (pp. 659–668). Walnut Creek, CA: Left Coast Press.

Tamas, S. (2011). *Life after leaving: The remains of spousal abuse.* Walnut Creek, CA: Left Coast Press.

Thompson, P. (1978). *The voice of the past: Oral history.* Oxford, UK: Oxford University Press.

Trinh, T. M. (1989). *Woman, native, other: Writing postcoloniality and feminism.* Bloomington: Indiana University Press.

Trinh, T. M. (1991). *When the moon waxes red: Representation, gender and cultural politics.* New York, NY: Routledge.

Turner, V. (1986a). *The anthropology of performance.* New York, NY: Performing Arts Journal Publications.

Turner, V.. 1986b. Dewey, Dilthey, and drama: An essay in the anthropology of experience. In V. M. Turner & E. M. Bruner (Eds.), *The anthropology of experience* (pp. 33–44). Urbana: University of Illinois Press.

Ulmer, G. (1989). *Teletheory.* New York, NY: Routledge.

Van Maanen, J. (2011). *Tales of the field: On writing ethnography* (2nd ed.). Chicago, IL: University of Chicago Press.

Wenner, J. S. (2013, May 16). The new Dylan. *Rolling Stone: Special Collectors Edition: Bob Dylan: 40 Years of Rolling Stone Interviews,* pp. 8–29.

Wright, W. (1986). *Lillian Hellman: The image, the woman.* New York, NY: Simon & Schuster.

Wyatt, J., Gale, K., Gannon, S., & Davies, B, (2011). *Deleuze and collaborative writing: An immanent plane of composition.* New York, NY: Peter Lang,

Index

Note: In page references f indicates figures.

⑤SAGE research**methods**

The essential online tool for researchers from the world's leading methods publisher

Find exactly what you are looking for, from basic explanations to advanced discussion

More content and new features added this year!

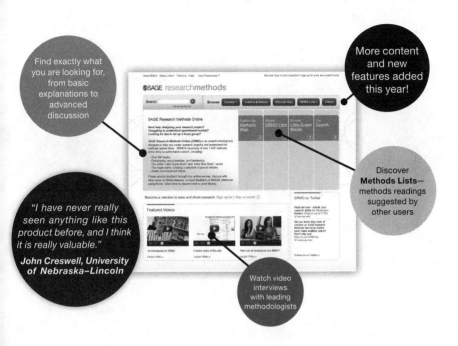

Discover **Methods Lists**—methods readings suggested by other users

"I have never really seen anything like this product before, and I think it is really valuable."

John Creswell, University of Nebraska–Lincoln

Watch video interviews with leading methodologists

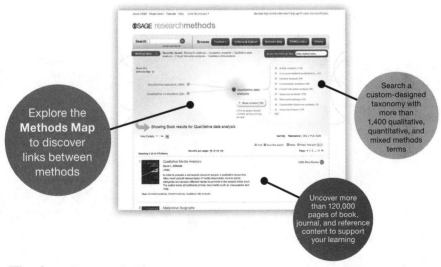

Search a custom-designed taxonomy with more than 1,400 qualitative, quantitative, and mixed methods terms

Explore the **Methods Map** to discover links between methods

Uncover more than 120,000 pages of book, journal, and reference content to support your learning

Find out more at
www.sageresearchmethods.com